THE GOOD LIFE

A MATTER OF CHOICE

Chapbook Press

Schuler Books
2660 28th Street SE
Grand Rapids, MI 49512
(616) 942-7330
www.schulerbooks.com

The Good Life: a Matter of Choice

ISBN 13: 9781948237352

Library of Congress Control Number: 2020903764

Copyright © 2020, Jerry Van Leeuwen
All rights reserved.

Artwork by Eleanor Vega

Cover Design by Lesley Van Leeuwen-Vega

No part of this book may be reproduced, scanned or distributed in any form without express permission of the copyright holder.

Printed in the United States by Chapbook Press.

I dedicate this book to my wife, Barbara, who stands by me in turbulent times and gives me her unconditional support and love; to my daughters, Lesley and Libby, my inspiration and purpose; and my many patients who have allowed me to help them make better trades in their lives and to enhance the growth of my own.

* * *

The author would like to express special thanks
to the following people:

Barb Van Leeuwen for initial editing, re-writing and general encouragement; Lesley Van Leeuwen-Vega for the cover design, layout, editing and insightful re-writing; Lazaro Vega for his suggestions, editing and typing; Eleanor Vega for creation of the characters used throughout the book and on the poster. Also thanks to Libby Ferin for her talents regarding sales and distribution; John Ferin for his recommendations; Alan Eggleston for his patient assistance with editing; and Maureen Shirey for many hours spent in typing and the initial setup for this book.

FOREWORD

Why did I decide to write this book?

As many of us approach what is likely the final third or even quarter of our lives, it's very easy to wish that we could go back, do things differently, communicate differently and have different outcomes. If I could go back, how different my life might have been.

I was raised in a dysfunctional environment fueled by alcohol. My own behavior was formed and molded in that tainted atmosphere. Understanding all my warts and poor choices at the end of most days, many years ago, helped me formulate a health strategy for living a better life: the good life. I began to realize the importance of making healthy trades of my life every day so that I wouldn't regret the price I paid. I became aware in my therapy how important it is to be in control of your private critic, to challenge negative thoughts and to not give anyone what I call your emotional credit card.

My own life's journey and choices, both good and bad, helped me gain insight that has led to my present therapeutic focus.

Over the past twenty-five years, it has been suggested by my patients (clients) that I should write a book about my philosophy of life. Finally, I have.

This book is intended to be a road map. Hopefully, it will assist you in making good trades each day on your life journey.

TABLE OF CONTENTS

CHAPTER 1
IN THE BEGINNING...4
Case Study #1...8
Case Study #2...11
Case Study #3...12

CHAPTER 2
WHAT IS A GOOD RELATIONSHIP?....................................20
Case Study #4...23
Case Study #5...26

CHAPTER 3
THE JOURNEY..28
Relationship Agreement..31
What Love Does...40

CHAPTER 4
WHO'S RESPONSIBLE FOR HOW I'M FEELING?................44

CHAPTER 5
WHY CAN'T I FEEL MORE WORTHWHILE?.........................50

CHAPTER 6
SO WHAT IF I'M INADEQUATE?..58
I CAN NEVER MEASURE UP SO WHY TRY?........................59
WHY WAIT FOR SOMEONE TO REJECT YOU?...................64

TABLE OF CONTENTS

CHAPTER 7
THE WORLD IS A STAGE..70

CHAPTER 8
BEHAVIOR..74

CHAPTER 9
RISK..80
STAYING ANGRY..85

CHAPTER 10
STRESS..88
Dr. Jerry's Rules..96
THE END - IS THIS TRIP REALLY OVER?..99
WHAT ARE YOU WAITING FOR?..112

YOU ARE GOING TO DIE.

I'm going to die, too. Therefore, it's not about dying.
It's about living and the quality of life we have while we're here.

There are no do-overs. So, where do we start?
The answer is here and now, but in order to do so,
it's important that we look at the beginning.

CHAPTER 1

Life...
That it will never come again
is what makes life so sweet.

- Emily Dickinson, American poet

THE GOOD LIFE: A MATTER OF CHOICE

IN THE BEGINNING

The beginning appears to be the best place to start when discussing nearly anything, especially us humans and how our behaviors and thought patterns are developed and exhibited as we journey through life.

Otto Rank, a Neo-Freudian (or a disciple/student of Freud), once said that the most difficult time in life is being born. We basically come out of a nurturing, warm and secure environment into one of extreme change. Perhaps our first memory may be of someone turning us upside down and slapping us on the behind. From that time we begin to grow and experience thousands, millions of statements and behaviors that are responsible for forming our own perceptions of self and the way we behave.

In our first few years, the messages we begin to develop for ourselves can come from the way we are touched or not touched by a parent or family member. It could be the touch of warmth, unconditional affection and love, or, conversely, avoidance of closeness through anger and hostility, physical or verbal abuse or simply emotional and physical withdrawal. The messages that a child hears during their formative years are extremely important. The child has no other perception or affirmation of self other than that which is given to them by their parents or parent figures and siblings, both verbally and nonverbally. If the message is, "I'm not happy with you," "I'm not happy with the way you act," or "I don't like you for doing that," that message can become a part of the self-perception of the child in a variety of ways, especially if the message is repetitive. How different if the parent repeats, "I'm not happy with you when you act that way, but I still care about you and love you"?

When a kid feels at an early age that he or she doesn't measure

In The Beginning

up, is a disappointment, or the expectations of important others are greater than what he/she is able to achieve, it can influence him or her. Whether it influences that person in a negative or a positive way depends on how the expectations are related and how they are received. Other messages that can reinforce this perception are, "Why can't you ever do anything right? Why can't you do what you're told? I don't like you for doing that," or other devaluative statements. The information that truly needs to be shared is, "I'm not happy when you don't do the things you are asked to do, or when you do things that are not acceptable, but I still accept *you*."

Other messages, such as, "Why can't you be like your brother or your sister, or even Max, the golden retriever?" and "If it wasn't for you, I could be... or we could be..." put the responsibility for a person's immediate or temporary unhappiness, unpleasantness or discomfort directly on the shoulders of the child.

Happily, when the message is one of unconditional love, acceptance and support, the young person, at a very early age, begins to see himself or herself as a unique and important individual. Again, in essence the message is, "I don't like what you did but I still love and care about you." That message separates the behavior from the individual so the youngster realizes they can do something about the behavior and that the behavior is not invasive. Dr. Rene Spitz, an expert on ego development (and a follower of Sigmund Freud who psychoanalyzed Freud), felt the first two years of life, and the messages we hear until age five, were the most important in establishing the foundations for one's perception of self. If the messages are,

"I'm so happy to have you," "You're a wonderful baby/child," "I love you just because you are you," "It is nothing to worry about," "It's okay," "You're such a special person," they are messages that affirm in a very positive way the individual and their perception of self. They also help establish individuality and not a comparison to someone or something.

As a young person grows, he or she is continually bombarded with messages that can reinforce a positive, or more problematically, a negative perception of self. These are messages such as, "Don't talk back," "Don't question me," "Speak only when spoken to," "You don't know what you're saying," "You're too young to have an opinion," "Don't be stupid," or "If you don't know what you're talking about, don't say anything." The behavioral result of these kinds of critical and unhealthy messages is often one of a less-assertive or even non-assertive approach to life. Specifically in the ways an individual will express themselves in later years, and how they may not be willing to test their adequacy in a number of areas. It is empirically better for the youngster when the messages are more positive and encouraging, for instance, "What do you think about that?," "That's interesting," "It certainly is another way to look at it," and "I like that."

If the negative messages a young person receives continue through childhood are reinforced by teachers who repeatedly say things like, "You don't understand," or "You don't have the right answer," and are accompanied by teacher impatience or an avoidance to call on them, the messages become either a verbal or nonverbal transaction informing the student that they aren't very bright or what they have to say isn't very important. Testing in school and the importance placed on grades and numerical scores for GPAs, ACTs, SATs and more only further serve to define the child's worth based on performance and not on their own inherent value. This is especially true if he or she is not able to perform to an expected level – due to any number of reasons – which may have nothing to do with their actual knowledge or ability. The end result is the same. Negative perception may be further enhanced by peer responses, lack of inclusion at parties, sporting events, weekend outings, and so on.

In my generation, even television added to one's positive or negative sense of self. For instance, if you answered a question posed on a game show or spoke out about a news story, someone else in the room might laugh at an incorrect answer or negatively comment on what they considered to be a flawed point of view. That's punishing. A more current example might be the kind of attention one receives on various social media platforms that can negatively reinforce one's self perception by allowing a person to feel devalued – from not being "liked" quite enough to suffereing the virutal attacks of trolling. This will usually reinforce an individual's non-assertiveness – to keep others from knowing what one thinks or feels – which helps avoid being criticized or discounted. It's a deflection. Thus begins the development of our "Private Critic" – what we say to ourselves, about ourselves, in relation to people or situations. In other words, your Private Critic is kind of an equal-opportunity observer, there to deliver inner thoughts of either a positive/self-affirming or negative/self-defeating nature.

Indecisiveness many times can be closely related to non-assertiveness. Non-assertiveness, in turn, may lead to the choice of a partner in a relationship who is very much the opposite – one who is highly assertive, domineering and even critical, who may make decisions for the non-assertive individual, freeing him or her from having to choose wrongly and being called out for it. After time, the dominant partner may lose respect for the passive one and treat him or her even more poorly, leading to more negative and unhealthy behavior, which in turn leads to more criticism from the dominant partner... and so on. The negativism creates its own cycle.

It's these messages or "scripts" that influence our private critic in either a negative or positive way. These private conversations decide whether we have a good or bad "trade" of our day. When each day is over, we look back and see – did we trade our time for something gratifying and enjoyable, or for something unhappy and emotionally upsetting? We will never experience that day over again so it's very important that we empower ourselves to make sure that, at the end of it, we feel confident that it was a good trade of our time – no matter how many negative or upsetting situations we were exposed to.

"Scripts" are incredibly powerful messages, either verbal or nonverbal, that individuals experience and are conditioned to play out in their lives – most of which can be quite positive and emotionally healthy. However, there are some scripts that are really counterproductive to emotionally satisfying lives and relationships. The following case studies provide some examples.

CASE STUDY #1

One case history of mine involved a young woman, thirty-four years of age, who was having extreme difficulties with her marital relationship as well as relationships with others. She came to see me as her husband was requesting a divorce. Her script throughout her life had been that she must be perfect in everything she did, or something ominous could occur and/or she would receive some kind of punishment. As a child, if her room was not cleaned up perfectly, she would be punished, both emotionally and sometimes physically. If her clothes were not found to be in ultra-organized order in her drawers, or not hanging neatly in her closet and matched according to color, something bad was going to happen.

This woman excelled academically but if she received an A- instead of an A, she could be found going into the throes of depression and would be sick with anticipatory anxiety over having to explain to her mother and father why she did not work harder to get the A. As she dressed for school as a young person, no matter what she put on to wear, or how nice she felt she looked, her mother often insisted that she change her clothes because they were not properly color coordinated and that represented poor parenting.

At age twenty-four, while obtaining her master's degree in college, she met a young man. She was able to mask her anxiety surrounding perfection most of the time, not allowing it to significantly interfere with the relationship, and she was married at age twenty-five. Her husband's line of work required him to travel a great deal and he was not aware of the severity of her struggles. He would make comments about coming home to a house that looked like something out of a magazine as nothing was ever out of place, and he complimented her on working so hard to keep it looking that way. He appreciated that guests loved eating meals in their home as everything was always excellently prepared and presented.

What he did begin to experience difficulty with was the amount of time she would spend in the bathroom, attempting to achieve perfection before leaving the house. This was then extended to fastidiousness in dressing their daughter, or how their daughter's room had to look, or how her daughter needed to take care of her toys. Although this client had sought treatment at various times, and was able to alleviate some of her symptoms of anxiety through medication, she was never able to eliminate the damaging effects they were having on herself and those she was connected to.

As her problems continued to become more serious and her symptoms more anxiety-provoking, her husband began to complain about the length of time it would take her to prepare a meal and he even started ordering take-out rather than waiting for dinner to be finished. They began missing scheduled events and movies because of how long she would spend getting ready, and their daughter was starting to grow critical of other children. Finally there came a severe confrontation after her husband found himself being woken in the middle of the night so that she could straighten the sheets that were wrinkled from sleeping. He could no longer tolerate her behavior and not only requested a divorce but custody of their daughter as well.

After an intense social history review and some testing, together we formulated a therapeutic plan to rewrite the script and act upon the revision, which she agreed to do. In talking to her husband, it was decided that he would hold off an any legal action regarding their marriage for at least ninety days to give her a chance to work on changing her behavior.

Her treatment plan was a three-pronged approach which included rescripting, behavior modification, and desensitization. The rescripting involved us taking a look at a number of earlier life experiences to search out when these obsessive behaviors began and what outside influences were dictating them. Behavior modification and desensitization acted as two sides of the same coin. With the former, she would make it a practice to be in the physical presence of things that upset her – a pile of newspapers or dishes in the sink – and work to tolerate those disturbances for short periods of time. Fifteen minutes. A half an hour. The latter treatment worked in a similar way, but involved her imagining these disturbances. She would "visit" an issue of anxiety and stress – again, perhaps a bed pillow out of place – and then return to a pleasant, restful scene in her head. She would repeat the action with a slightly more bothersome issue and return back to that place of calm. Note: the restful scene was not to be based on cleanliness or the like. Instead, it was beautiful park or beach of her choosing. Something that purposely didn't involve that kind of control. We continued to work in these areas, pushing the boundaries a bit further with each session, and she was very dedicated to making progress. In this case, she was actually able to use her perfectionistic obsessionalism in a proactive manner, with positive results. In a relatively short period of time, she began to gain insight regarding her behavior and was able to identify the personally devaluative aspects of such, and implement change when she saw it occurring.

Over the next several weeks she showed improvement in her presenting problem areas and was able to continue eliminating and/or alleviating areas that were disruptive to both her relationship and her parenting. We worked together until we both agreed that she was decidedly in control of her self-defeating scripts and finally, treatment was terminated on a call-back basis.

Since that time I have received a Christmas card every year from her family. Three years ago, I even received a card from her daughter who is now married and has a child of her own. What I find most revealing is that my patient always signs her name by spelling it wrong and including a little smiley face next to it.

CASE STUDY #2

Cases #2 and #3 both involved spouses, primarily females, who allowed themselves to be subjected to emotional and/or physical abuse in family relationships. In this first case, a wife came in to see me after her fourth physical abuse encounter with her husband. Her primary intent was to try to understand what she was doing or not doing that caused her husband to act the way he did.

Her script revealed that she came out of an extremely emotionally and physically abusive environment where her parents would displace their own aggression toward one another on their children. Her mother vented anger and animosity at having to stay in an unhappy marital relationship by blaming it on the fact that her daughter had been born. Her father behaved in similar terms, saying that if it wasn't for his children, he'd have the money to do the things he wanted to do and could afford to leave his wife.

She grew up feeling that her parents' angst was due to her very existence and she worked tirelessly to do whatever she could to please them so that they would not be so disappointed and upset. Additionally, she made it a point not to ask for anything or make plans to go anywhere in order to reduce the expenses that seemed to burden her father. She remembered rushing home from school to do the washing and ironing and clean the house so that her mother would not feel taken advantage of.

Almost all of the relationships she was involved with were verbally, and many times physically, abusive to her. She ultimately married a man who offered many of the same characteristics of her father, believing that if she could please her husband in ways that she was not able to please her father as a youngster, he would in turn offer her the kindness or acceptance that she never received. However, this thinking proved delusional on her part and all this man did was take advantage of her: she worked very hard and turned over all of her money to him for *his* wants, such as drinking and shopping. She didn't recall going anywhere together, such as out to dinner or to a movie, although he always seemed to be out somewhere and spending money.

When she finally began to gain insight into the origin of her behavior – based on the devaluative and demeaning script that she grew up with – she was able to start working therapeutically in rewriting that script. She saw that she had grown up believing that her validation came from *performing* and *doing*, not *thinking* and *being*. As our discussions progressed, it became evident to her that this kind of validation had never really worked and she moved toward the reality of what *is* and not what *was* – toward a new and healthier way of gaining love and acceptance. She ultimately disengaged herself from the destructive relationship, which also necessitated her obtaining a Personal

Protection Order from the courts on her soon-to-be ex-husband.

A few years later she met an emotionally healthy and kind man whom she ultimately married. She had experienced enough revision of her previous script that she now believed she deserved good treatment. She continued to do positive things for her new husband on a regular basis and found them to be reciprocated, and she felt deserving of such. The last time I spoke with her, she appeared to be gratifying her needs and enjoying the environment in which she found herself. Additionally, she felt that for the first time she was able to truly focus on being a responsible and loving parent to her two children.

CASE STUDY #3

A forty-eight year old woman came into my office recounting a very impaired relationship with her significant other and wanted to know what she could do to improve it. Her social history revealed that this was her fourth marriage and that each of her marriages had been with an alcoholic.

She grew up as an only child in an environment with a violent alcoholic father and observed him being physically abusive to her mother on numerous occasions. She would attempt to rectify whatever he was upset about, to avoid his explosive behavior, and this would work occasionally but not often. She could not remember receiving any affection or positive statements from her father, although she tried desperately to gain his acknowledgment and affirmation.

After leaving home and going off to college, she became involved in relationships that offered many of the same characteristics. She maintained a belief that if she married a man and she was all the things he needed her to be, he would ultimately quit his drinking and respond to her in ways that she had always desired and never experienced from her childhood. This was fantastic thinking on her part as these individuals never fulfilled her wishes, instead offering her the same negative experience she had growing up.

Through her involvement in therapy, she saw that she had repeatedly surrounded herself with "takers" while she worked to be the perpetual "giver." And until she began setting up healthy boundaries, working to be more empowered, she would continue to be drawn to the same kind of person in any future relationships. She couldn't depend on anyone else for her own happiness any longer – true acceptance could only come from within. As we worked together, she gained enough strength and insight to challenge her current spouse and give him an ultimatum. Either he would get involved in treatment or she would divorce him. He chose treatment and maintained sobriety, as well as working through relationship counseling to the point of improving the quality of their relationship, their lives together and the lives of their children. Until changed, this was one more case of an individual living out their script which had resulted in bad trades of each and every day.

* * *

As we can see in these case studies, when a person is brought up in a family where there is strong emphasis on negative perfectionistic messages like, "If you're going to do it, do it right or not at all," or "Don't be satisfied with what you've done, you can always do better," and so on, a youngster may begin to perceive the importance of life as being one that equates success and happiness with perfection. Not only will they continue to be very critical and demanding of themselves, but they usually carry those same standards into their treatment of others. In their cases, no matter how well one performs a task, an assignment at school, a job, or even throws a party, they always feel they could have done better, never accepting that what they have done is just fine. Never acknowledging that if they would like to improve upon whatever it is they have just accomplished, they can do that some other day. They may fail to realize that whether or not it could have been better isn't really the issue; that perhaps it was the best they could do at that particular time and it doesn't represent their worth as a person. When caught in this cycle of dissatisfaction with self, even if someone says, "You did a great job!" the flatterer may instead be perceived as wanting something from them or simply not knowing what they're talking about.

The unhealthy perception of self is put into a knapsack of self doubt that we drag along with us in all situations in where we need to test our adequacy – whether it be employment, school, dating, athletics or anything in which performance is put on an emotional rating scale.

If the messages an individual receives while growing up equate to their performance, that same sack of unpleasantness may be carried with them until death, unless a new choice is made: importance as an individual should in no way be equated with how well (or not well) one may do something.

Let me repeat that: your worth is NOT, and should never be, tied to your success.

When we haven't performed as well as we would have liked to – for whatever reason – it's healthy for us to feel sad or disappointed. But in no way should we perceive ourselves as being less than who we are because of it.

In my practice, I've seen so many of these scripts prove extremely counter-productive to a healthy relationship with a significant other. In the earlier example where one individual made her bed partner get up during the middle of the night so she could straighten the sheets, her action was the result of the devaluative behavior she had experienced as a child by her mother when making her bed. Another situation involved her as a hostess who needed everything to be so perfect for a dinner party that by the time the dinner was served, the food was overdone. Their visitors had also become so restless that they filled up on appetizers and weren't interested in eating the meal, sending the hostess the message that they didn't even like it. Of course, this only made her determined to do a better job the next time, snowballing the self-critical behavior and increasing anxiety for herself and her family.

The reality is, we are all human; we are fallible and imperfect: we screw up. That's just part of life. We all have about a 20 percent mess-up factor, which may or may not figure into any given situation, but if it does, we are better off to address the mess and just fix it if we can, without putting our worth, or the value of who we are on the line. Fix it or forget about it.

Messages received while growing up can be insidious. Although the parents may in no way perceive themselves as non-loving, they might make a suggestion after their child cuts the lawn, or performs some other task, without first giving any positive reinforcement at all. Not saying a word, they may clean off areas of the car after their daughter has just washed it, or wipe up the countertops after their son has cleaned the kitchen. Wouldn't it be more helpful—and perhaps more kind—to say, "Nice job, I really appreciate it. In the future I wonder if you would consider..."?

Whether spoken or not, these negative messages are internalized. And no matter what the child does, they don't measure up in the eyes of the people they deem most important. That leads to the choice that they must always do better and try harder to please. There are millions of people who spend their entire lives in people-pleasing mode in an effort to be approved of, or accepted, trying to avoid having anyone say anything negative or unkind about them. They fundamentally give up on being loved or cared for by others and in doing so may pay the price of never testing their adequacy in any number of situations due to the inordinate amount of energy they spend on others.

Certainly, this is not to suggest that it's unhealthy to please someone else or to do someone a kindness, but it relates to the critical choices one makes. If the choice a person makes is that they would really enjoy doing whatever for someone else because it feels good to them and fits their need, then that's a good thing. However, if the doing of something for someone else is so that one will be accepted or approved of, then it becomes an unhealthy behavior. So it's all about context here: whatever one does may be appropriate, as long as it doesn't violate the individual or does not violate self in the doing of it.

Changing one's perception of self and exhibiting more healthy and appropriate behavior is found in the choices we make – and that includes challenging our unhealthy and, many times, destructive belief systems. The life a person *learns with* does not have to be the life they continue to choose to *live*. It can change. It can change if they are willing to take the risk and challenge their belief system by honestly assessing the proof they have for the way they feel and perceive themselves to be. So much of the time, we lose control of our private critic, that little voice in our head that either negates us or affirms us, and those things we tell ourselves, about ourselves, with no supporting evidence need to be discarded curbside – like the trash on Thursday morning.

We always have a choice, no matter how difficult it may appear to be. Every hour, every day – we have the power to choose how we wish to react to anyone or anything.

CHAPTER 2

Getting along.
Really.

THE GOOD LIFE: A MATTER OF CHOICE

WHAT IS A GOOD RELATIONSHIP?

Whoever taught any of us how to have a relationship? Most of us have had more formal training on how to drive a car, putt a little ball into a hole or even brush our teeth than how to understand the most successful ways to care for the significant relationships in our lives. Yet we wonder why nearly all of us stumble emotionally and experience difficulties that continue to result in disappointments – and sometimes even contribute to ending those very relationships we thought would be a fundamental part of our existence until we died.

There is incredible confusion in our society regarding what a good relationship really looks like. Relationships that are seen in the movies or on television are often either devaluative and demeaning, or fanciful, and not, as a rule, rooted in reality. If you haven't had good modeling throughout your formative years or are not connected with individuals who exhibit healthy relationships, it can be very difficult to understand a healthy relationship actually looks like.

Most people focus on open, honest communication, respect, unconditional support, compliments, affection, and an attempt to understand what makes the other feel special and a priority in the relationship. However, many of us also think of a good relationship as being with someone who is physically attractive, wants to spend lots of time with us, strives to understand what is going on in our life, and who is, night after night, interested in experiencing over-the-edge intimacy with us. Hmm. When this doesn't occur in real life, one partner in the relationship – or both – usually begins to exhibit disappointment.

Obviously not everyone expresses the same needs or desires that result in a relationship of specialness and prioritization, but things such as honest communication, affection and support are important and significant in developing the emotional, spiritual and physical connections that make relationships a priority in our lives.

We choose to marry our significant other and our expectation, as a rule, is a continuation of our dating experiences – which is one more way of fooling ourselves into believing that there will be negligible changes. We then encounter a variety of new challenges, such as caring for a house, bringing up children, social commitments, extended family demands, and a host of other obligations and events that occupy our time in a way for which we were not prepared. Both individuals usually have so many other responsibilities that beckon for their time that they simply cannot allocate the same number of hours they did back when they were dating, and the focus was clearly on one another. We then wonder why we have problems.

It's not that we don't want to have successful relationships, or that we aren't willing to try in whatever ways we can to make them happen, but we bring to those relationships unhealthy scripts or conditional behaviors that prevent us from prioritizing our relationship as a significant responsibility – our significant responsibility. Some of the most important aspects in creating and maintaining a successful relationship are when both parties do whatever they can, even with those other demands, to gratify their partner emotionally, physically and spiritually. If your partner would like you to sing "Hey Jude" once a week, you had better learn the words. If your partner would like some chocolate chip cookies, you need to get out the dough. If they want it and it doesn't violate you in some way, you might want to figure out a way to do it. And they need to do the same for you. The goal here is always prioritize the relationship and make sure your partner feels special. We recognize there are many other interferences or commitments vying for your time. But it doesn't take much to put a sticky note on the rearview mirror saying, "Guess who loves you?" or make a twenty second phone call just to say, "I wondered how your day is going and I can't wait to see you later."

There are many factors that exemplify a successful relationship, but three of the most important are:

1.) Do whatever is necessary to personally be as emotionally healthy as possible.
2.) Always be willing to flex and compromise, where you can.
3.) Be unconditionally committed to do whatever you can to make your partner feel special, and to feel as if he or she is a priority (as long as it doesn't violate either person).

A good litmus test in any healthy relationship should be that each partner goes to bed at night convinced that their life is significantly better because the other person is in it.

As mentioned earlier, most of us fantasize that getting married or becoming committed in a permanent relationship with a significant other will just be a continuation of our dating experiences. Unfortunately, the reality of the difference appears far too quickly and is, for many, much too disappointing. Perhaps the healthier choice is not to marry the person you think you can live with, but marry the person you feel you can't live without. We believe, usually mistakenly, that marriage will simply involve spending more time doing what already enjoy doing – talking until the wee hours with open and spontaneous displays of affection and intimacy. We may not anticipate the number of pressures surrounding the marital relationship: extended family, children, financial matters, health issues and more. Awareness sets in that neither partner can be on their best behavior or in tip-top shape 24/7, even though this may have seemed to be the reality while in their dating mode. The following case studies provide some interesting examples.

CASE STUDY #4

I counseled a couple who came in to see me several years ago because they were no longer happy in their marital arrangement and had decided that they would go in separate directions to fulfill their respective needs. They'd been married for thirty-two years and had raised three children who were all leading healthy and successful lives of their own.

In exploring their history, it became quite apparent that they had been spending their time parenting their children and developing their individual careers, and had made the assumption that their relationship would take care of itself. This, unfortunately, is a situation that is not uncommon with many couples once their children have left the home to move on to new lives.

In spending time with each of them one-on-one and then together, it was apparent that although they were respectful and acted responsibly toward one another, they were not communicative and they neglected to inform one another of their needs and desires, as well as what would make each of them feel like more of a priority to their partner. In a session where we were all together, each of them were asked to be open and honest regarding these types of feelings, which generated quite a pause for both. They didn't appear to be insightful of these concerns regarding their partner. When the wife said, "For the last twenty-five years I've just hated it when you passionately kiss my ear and neck during the times when we're intimate," the husband responded by throwing up his arms, looking at me and saying, "Gee, Doc, and here I thought that had been a real turn-on for her all this time!"

They gained insight into the possibility that the problem was not that each of them couldn't be the partner the other wanted – but that they might carry the same behaviors into their next relationship and would most likely receive the same results. Whether they decided to terminate the relationship was their choice, but another option could be to take the next sixty days during which they ask one another at the end of each day if there was anything he or she could have done – or anything their spouse would like them to do – to increase satisfaction in the relationship. Additionally, it was recommended that they make the effort to communicate about the things they each really found to be satisfying socially, recreationally and intimately.

They tried this and within a short period of time began to feel genuinely more connected to one another. An epilogue to this case was that they continue to do the homework they agreed upon, and they remain together in their relationship. And they have told me that they still set a time almost every day to discuss one another's needs.

The good news is that progress does not have to cease just because one raises the bar significantly on their commitment to each other. There's no satisfaction ceiling here. If both individuals were to ask, if not daily then at least a regular basis, what they could do to make one another feel special or enhance the other's quality of their life, they might find their emotional and physical needs being met in spite of all of the other stressful interferences and extenuating circumstances. Many couples come into my relationship sessions stating that either he or she (or both) are not the same person they were back when they were dating. This reminds me of what philosopher and psychologist William James once said. He stated that all couples are six personalities: what he thinks he is, what she thinks he is, and what he really is, along with what she thinks she is, what he thinks she is, and what she really is.

Not surprisingly, many problems occur over time in a relationship, after two become married or, in effect, permanently committed. As the Greek philosopher Epictetus said, "Difficulties are things that show a person what they are." Once committed, there is often a more lackadaisical approach to the relationship, and the couple begins not only taking the relationship for granted, but not exhibiting the best "he" or "she" to the other, as they had in the dating experience. Quality time isn't allocated, the ability to listen to each other is sporadic at best, and displays of attention or affection become limited. Perhaps that is why you hear so many people say that their partner is "not the person I married" or, "you certainly didn't act that way when we were dating." It's also important to remember that every day we experience a growth in self and we don't all grow at the same rates of speed.

In addition to not presenting the best self to your partner, the most prevalent self-defeating behavior is the one of "condition." In most relationships, couples move from the dating-compromising-flexible focus to one of conditionality, which is usually more of an "I'm not going to do that for him because he didn't do this for me" or, "I don't intend to go along with what she wants because she hasn't gone along with what I've requested" kind of attitude. Taking this approach, the two parties continue to behave in an "if/then" way, building up points against the other that they can use to rationalize, or to even exhibit significant anger and withdrawal. As stated before, in any successful relationship, both parties need to be as emotionally healthy as they are capable of being and be willing to compromise and flex. That underscores the primary unconditional commitment to the relationship: no matter what the other person may or may not be doing, as long as you are in a committed relationship or marriage, it's your responsibility to do whatever you can – without compromising yourself – to prioritize the other person and make him or her feel special. Being unwilling to do this and believing the relationship will get better is like believing you can win the lottery without buying a ticket.

THE GOOD LIFE: A MATTER OF CHOICE

CASE STUDY #5

Another case I can recall involved a couple who came in with the plan to divorce, as both of them had recently had an affair. While exploring the reasons behind their violation of the relationship, both seemed to believe that their partner was no longer interested in them, their ideas, or in spending time with them. This occurred over a long period of time and instead of challenging one another regarding these concerns, their vulnerabilities led them each to connect with someone outside the relationship who appeared to enjoy their company more and show an interest in what was going on in their life.

It became readily apparent that each of them had connected with people who were both self-serving individuals in an effort for these new partners to meet their own needs at the expense of my clients. The history of their twenty-three year marriage revealed that they had each lived with these assumptions of indifference – and their infidelity was just another reaction to these assumptions – without ever challenging whether they held any validity. This is typical of so many couples. They become disenchanted and disengaged with their partner based on the assumption that the partner is no longer interested in their likes or desires. This usually turns out to be a basic lack of communication rather than the reality of their situation.

In spite of the hurt and emotional pain, this couple was willing to see that if they could turn the corner on their relationship and honestly debunk each assumption, they might be successful. Unfortunately, many who experience similar situations find it easier to move off in another direction as opposed to dealing with the emotional conflict they experience. These two understood that there's no "quick fix" in any relationship and accepted the belief that "we can never truly get it right, but we can get it better." They were able to view their relationship honestly as a journey with no fixed end point, but as one that welcomed and could benefit from continued improvement.

CHAPTER 3

Human felicity
is produced not so much
by great pieces of good fortune
that seldom happen,
as by little advantages
that occur every day.

- Benjamin Franklin

THE JOURNEY

When we're young, most of us operate under certain assumptions of denial: we're immortal; we're never going to die; our parents aren't going to die either; and of course, those same parents don't have sex. As we get older, we realize correctly that there's an end to everything and everybody. Instead of appreciating that insight and profound awareness, we waste so much of the precious life that we have going through depression, anxiety, worry, anger and many other emotional difficulties because of the choices that we make and the events that we encounter. For example, worry does nothing productive but it still manages to make an individual upset. Worry takes away quality of life, but it never changes the outcome. There are some who believe that worry is an unconscious superstition – if we worry about things, they won't occur. People might tell you they worried they wouldn't pass a test but got a B+, or worried about not going to the prom but ended up with two dates, or worried about a plane not arriving safely then disembarked after a pleasant flight. For many, this is a repetitive behavior practiced throughout the formative years well into adult life. People may have also observed the people they receive scripts from – parents or other role models – engaging in similar activities, which reinforced that same emotional thought process.

Whether depressed, stressed, worried, or in the throes of any emotionally taxing state of being, we can stop and challenge these situations and realize that the choice we're making may be interfering with or blocking completely our ability to experience good energy. And, again, it does not alter the outcome.

In a tribute to the state of wedlock entitled "Our Journey," an anonymous writer conveyed the following:

Our Journey

We've come a long way together
and now we're getting old and slow.
Bear with me a little longer, dear.
We don't have far to go.
We've had glad days and sad days
and some very scary mad days,
love days and hate days
and life is really great days,
dating days and wedding days,
then it's time for mating days.
Honey days, dear days,
some 'don't you dare come near' days.
Some hugging, kissing, touching days
and 'I love you very much' days.
Then child days; those wild days
and always feeling riled days.
Those lazy, dazy, crazy,
you truly do amaze me days.
There were short days and those long days
when everything goes wrong days.
Sunny days and funny days
and mighty short of money days.
Yay days and nay days
and anything you say days.
Cheerful days, and those tearful
when I really got an earful days.
Restful days and questful days
and a lot of really stressful days.
Tough days, rough days
and those 'I've had enough' days.

THE GOOD LIFE: A MATTER OF CHOICE

Lots of gay days and play days;
but that was in our heydays.
Some Mondays and fun days
and other more to come days!
Also there were a bunch of really dumb days;
the glum days; the turn your back and hum days.
The wham, bam, slam days;
'take me as I am' days,
grouchy days, ouchy days,
the moping on the couchy days.
The sigh days, cry days,
I think I want to die days.
The baby days, the balky days,
the sulky, sulky, sulky days.
Then comes the 'I'd like to make amends' days
and the joy of being friends days.

Now to view our life objectively, I hope you do agree:
we've lived a pretty normal life and had a love abundantly.
Though we've come a long way together, to me you're not old or slow.
Please hold my hand as we go onward, we don't have far to go.

    This tribute speaks of love and perseverance, and an acceptance of those experiences that are normal interactions of individuals who find themselves living together on a daily basis. Living in a society where the responsibility of ownership is becoming more estranged as a part of human existence with the passing of no-fault accidents and no-fault divorces, etc., it seems that no one out there wants to assume the responsibility of what behavioral constructs lead to unpleasant events. In relationships of commitment and marriage and living or being together, it's imperative we understand that this is a journey: we must continuously work on improving the quality of our love and unconditional commitment to each other.

To understand areas that need to be focused on for improvement, a Relationship Agreement can sometimes be helpful. For most of the clients who seek relationship assistance, I usually develop an agreement that gives them an ongoing road map to follow – not only to deal with the specific relationship issues they are experiencing, but to also help them gain new awareness for future problem solving. An example follows for John and Jane:

<u>Relationship Agreement for John and Jane</u>

John will be more open and honest with Jane. *(i.e., needs, feelings, etc.)*	Jane will be more open and honest with John. *(i.e., needs, feelings, etc.)*
John will greatly improve his assertiveness with Jane.	Jane will greatly improve her assertiveness with John.
John will allocate more quality time with Jane.	Jane will allocate more quality time with John.
John will greatly improve his compromising behavior with Jane.	Jane will greatly improve her compromising behavior with John.
John will greatly reduce his TV watching.	Jane will greatly improve her decision making in all areas.

THE GOOD LIFE: A MATTER OF CHOICE

John will greatly improve his initiation of activities with Jane and with family functions.	Jane will greatly improve her saying "no" when appropriate.
John will initiate more affection and sexual intimacy with Jane.	Jane will initiate more affection and sexual intimacy with John.
John will initiate more loving behavior toward Jane. *(i.e., positive attitude, respect, patience, consideration, tolerance, support, cooperation, appreciation, etc.)*	Jane will initiate more loving behavior toward John. *(i.e., positive attitude, respect, patience, consideration, tolerance, support, cooperation, appreciation, etc.)*
John will expend more energy using the "I" in conversations.	Jane will expend more energy using the "I" in conversations.
John will greatly improve his listening skills when Jane is communicating.	Jane will greatly improve her listening skills when John is communicating.
John will greatly improve his nighttime boundaries out of the home.	Jane will greatly improve her nighttime boundaries out of the home.
John will greatly improve his honesty with Jane in all areas.	Jane will greatly improve her honesty with John in all areas.
John will expend more energy socially and recreationally in areas of Jane's interests.	Jane will expend more energy socially and recreationally in areas of John's interests.

John will initiate more social and recreational activities with other couples.

Jane will initiate more social and recreational activities with other couples.

John will initiate more social and recreational activities with members of the same sex.

Jane will initiate more social and recreational activities with members of the same sex.

John will expend more energy dealing with the "here and now."

Jane will expend more energy dealing with the "here and now."

John will eliminate his assumptions of Jane.

Jane will eliminate her assumptions of John.

John will greatly improve his flexibility regarding discussions and decisions with Jane.

Jane will greatly improve her flexibility regarding discussions and decisions with John.

John will establish one date night per week with Jane.

Jane will establish one date night per week with John.

John will greatly improve his involvement with Jane regarding domestic chores.

Jane will greatly improve her self-concept, self-esteem and self-confidence through therapy and other sources.

John will greatly improve his sensitivity regarding Jane's concerns.

Jane will greatly improve her sensitivity regarding John's concerns.

THE GOOD LIFE: A MATTER OF CHOICE

John will greatly improve his health habits in all areas.	Jane will greatly improve her health habits in all areas.
John will expend more energy giving positive strokes to Jane.	Jane will expend more energy giving positive strokes to John.
John will expend more energy exhibiting behavior from "his kid."	Jane will expend more energy exhibiting behavior from "her kid."

Undersigned:

_____   _____

John   Jane

Witness:

_____   _____

Jerry B. Van Leeuwen, PhD PC   Date

Although this isn't a legal document, it is an agreement which I recommend be taken out on a weekly to monthly basis for discussion, in an effort to ascertain whether there is anything either one of them is not doing or to identify a need for improvement in any area. The Relationship Agreement becomes a vehicle to focus on the "we," "our" and "us" aspects of the couple in the relationship. If either partner feels there are additional items that need to be added, that can be done, but it must always be done with an item added in each partner's column so that the Agreement maintains a balance.

When talking to couples, their response is usually something along the lines of, "We've been doing this so long, I don't think we can change" or, "That's just the way he or she is." In reality, most of the time it's the fear that the other person will be unable to succeed in carrying out what they've committed to doing. Televangelist and motivational speaker Dr. Robert Schuller once asked, "What great thing would you attempt if you knew you could not fail?" If you're not pre-occupied with envisioning the possibility of a negative outcome, or maintaining an irrational belief system and feeding your fears that you cannot become what your partner needs to have a successful relationship, what might you be willing to do instead? So many people find it easier to insist that they don't have a good partner, as opposed to figuring out what they need to do to better understand that individual and, in turn, help them become a better partner. These interpersonal problems have been with us since the beginning of time. It was Socrates, one of the founders of Western philosophy, who quipped, "By all means marry; if you get a good wife, you'll be happy. If you get a bad one, you'll become a philosopher." The only way one can ever truly fail is by not taking the risk to address and challenge their fear – because no matter what the outcome, you will always know that you did what you could to face what scared you, and that itself equals success.

    We all embark on a relationship with the idea that it is a good one with a good person. I don't believe that any of us would consciously disrupt or devalue our life by deciding, "Hey, I know! I'll throw away all the good things I have with this person in order to simply start over and be alone." That would be ludicrous, but in essence, that seems to be what so many people ultimately do. They find it easier to remain dissatisfied or unhappy than explore other options that could make both individuals feel more satisfied and more connected. And some would rather just move on in a new direction without having even attempted to make the changes necessary to improve the quality of their lives together; after all that is often easier. So many times we look at the negative aspects of what our partner is or cannot be, but how often do we explore all of the good things that he or she exhibits or the positive aspects he or she brings into our life? It certainly is a question we should all ask ourselves and one that can often generate a great deal of satisfaction.

A Personal Marital Contract first appeared in *Woman's Day* magazine on August 7, 1978, and we can still see how pertinent that contract remains decades later. It begs the question: have the areas of concern and disappointment that have always been part and parcel of impaired relationships been changed at all by the insights now available in books, online...just about everywhere? The answer is: only if we seek them out and choose to employ them. The Good Life is truly a matter of choice, and making healthy, responsible and loving choices in a committed relationship only serves to gratify both partners' needs in the highest manner possible. No matter the filter through which you choose to view your relationship – spiritual, emotional or philosophical – the gratification of your partner's needs (to whatever

level you can without violating or devaluing self), appears to be the most logical and self-serving decision you can make in committing to another person. And you can – and should – then expect the same consideration in return.

When hurtful and negative thinking occurs in relationships it's pretty difficult to feel happiness, enjoyment or contentment. We spend too much of our lives awful-izing, horrible-izing, terrible-izing, catastrophe-izing and immobilizing ourselves. This prevents us from utilizing each day as a gift and those around us as additional presents for which we can be happy and thankful. Changing our thinking on this will help us immensely in making a good trade of our day – no matter what we might encounter or whichever one of a hundred and forty seven things didn't happen exactly the way we might have liked it to.

Relationships are, simply put, a series of events and experiences, and while these experiences may not always be enjoyable or satisfying, perceiving them in a negative manner will only encourage the outcome to be more negative and unpleasant. As the saying goes, "If we wake up in the morning to a life that's full of lemons, let's grab a pitcher and start making lemonade." A healthy philosophy like that encourages us to embrace each day with the very best attitude we can. Certain behaviors help to make relationships far more successful, such as listening when your partner speaks and making your relationship emotionally safe by speaking to one another in respectful and gentle ways. Let your partner know what he or she is doing right and show appreciation. Surprise your partner, and allow the "kid" in both of you to experience fun together. Things to be avoided? Criticizing by bringing things up out of the past to create emotional upset in the present and scapegoating instead of owning responsibility for our own feelings.

Most important is to always give one another unconditional love. Love for your partner is not something doled out based on the day, your mood or your partner's behavior. It instead should be who you are, it should be your identity – with no less a commitment to your partner than to yourself. Anyone who's ever been in a relationship can tell you that love is easily said, but not easily done. "Doing" love means loving unconditionally and that's a choice that's available to each of us at any time.

As we continue to move forward in establishing a healthy relationship with our significant other, it becomes apparent that choices are available in every minute of the day. At any moment we can choose to adapt to change. As said by Pamela Crosby, a certified Life Coach and pastor, "I remember times when I've been in conflict with others. I wouldn't bend; I refused to meet the other person halfway; I was narrow minded. I felt right but unhappy. And then a light appeared in the form of someone who loved me and patiently waited for me to regroup, reassess, and discover within myself my greater capacity for love. We are surrounded by diversity. In order to make appropriate changes in behavior and values, we must risk. We must endure pain. But after the struggle comes renewal, renewal for those in conflict and for the ones who are used to light the way."

This relates to the metaphor put forth by Dr. John Gottman and his *Four Horsemen of Marriage*: Jealousy, Perfectionism, Possessiveness and Control. Just like the Four Horsemen of the Apocalypse – Conquest, War, Famine and Death – the relational Four Horsemen can do the same essential damage, and when more than one is operating, it always compounds the degree of difficulty and unhappiness for the other partner.

Take jealousy for example: instead of challenging the message, we create insecurities and we upset ourselves…but nothing changes. Jealousy is the result of one's insecurities – thinking that one is not important enough, pretty enough, smart enough. That kind of thinking causes an individual to make unhealthy choices about him or herself which can then pollute the way they respond to others. A case in point was a joke printed years ago in the *Reader's Digest* "Laughter is the Best Medicine" column: "A terribly jealous woman used to submit her husband to a regular inspection every evening. A small hair on his coat would lead to the most frightful of scenes. One night, finding nothing, she burst into tears and cried, 'Even bald women now?'"

On the control front, one of the major issues in the unhappiness between couples is their lack of playfulness and having fun with each other. They're so focused and committed to being adult or "parental" – and in control – they forget that the kid in each of them also needs to be nourished in order to make a greater connection and enable them to see that other person as their best friend. Isn't it interesting that most of us find it effortless to be fun and playful with our good friends, but when it comes to the one individual in our life who should be our best friend, that person often gets the least amount of attention, time or flexibility.

As I mentioned earlier, each night when both partners go to bed, they should be able to say to themselves that their life is so much better because the other person is a part of it. If either one or both isn't comfortable with that phrase, it can feel like there is an emotional specter hovering over him or her, ready to swoop down and interfere with the connection that's being taken for granted in the relationship. Again we say, "It's not about marrying the person you think you can live with, it's about marrying the person you feel you can't live without." That being said, every one of us is obliged to be introspective about what we're doing or not doing to fulfill that commitment.

Referenced by Dr. M. Scott Peck in *The Road Less Traveled* another way to phrase it is that when a person is considering becoming permanently involved with another, one of the most important decisions they need to make is to be unconditionally committed to enhancing that other individual's life.

A solid unconditional foundation – one that will help people endure and resolve difficulties and disagreements – is when both parties come into the relationship as emotionally healthy as they are capable of being, willing to be flexible and compromising. The commitment to one another is cheated by a partner who doesn't give the best he or she can be in that relationship. It's strengthened by the partner who refuses to allow anyone or anything to interfere with that commitment.

THE GOOD LIFE: A MATTER OF CHOICE

In *The Art of Living*, noted French writer Andre Maurois wrote, "A marriage without conflicts is almost as inconceivable as a nation without crises." And in *Thoughts in a Dry Season*, British writer Gerald Brenan wrote, "The great thing about marriage is that it enables one to be alone without feeling loneliness."

In a healthy relationship, your partner should always be there unconditionally to enhance your life and to gratify your needs – even at the times you feel alone. According to American psychiatrist David Viscott, "To love and be loved is to feel the sun from both sides." Though its origin is unknown, the following list illustrates several examples of what love does or doesn't do:

LOVE	LOVE DOESN'T
ACCEPTS you wherever you are.	ABUSE you or take you for granted.
AFFIRMS your goodness and giftedness.	ASK you to march to a different drummer.
CARES about you, wants to know that you're okay.	BLAME you or carry angry grudges.
CHALLENGES you to be all you can be.	BULLY you by anger, a loud voice or tears.
EMPATHIZES – knows what it's like to be you.	GET you into win-lose arguments.
ENCOURAGES you to believe in yourself.	GIVE you unsolicited advice.

LOVE

IS GENTLE in its way of
dealing with you.

KEEPS CONFIDENCES –
your secrets are safe.

IS KIND, always for you,
on your side.

LAUGHS A LOT,
always with, never at you.

LOOKS FOR GOODNESS
in you and finds it.

MAKES YOU FEEL GLAD
that you're you.

OVERLOOKS your foolish
vanities, human weaknesses.

PRAYS for your needs and
your growth.

SEES good things in you
that others had never noticed.

LOVE DOESN'T

JUDGE you or tell you
"what your whole trouble is."

JUST TOLERATE you as
a condescending favor.

MAKE YOU PROVE
yourself, again and again.

NEED always to be right,
to have all the answers.

POUT or refuse to talk to you.

PUNISH you for being wrong.

REMEMBER all the things
you have done wrong.

SEEK and call attention
to itself.

SHOW OFF, just to let you
know where you stand.

THE GOOD LIFE: A MATTER OF CHOICE

LOVE

SHARES itself with you, by self-disclosure.

SPEAKS UP when you need someone to defend you.

IS TACTFUL even when confronting you.

TAKES RESPONSIBILITY for its own behavior.

TELLS YOU THE TRUTH always and honestly.

THINKS about you and your needs.

IS TOUGH OR TENDER, depending on your needs.

UNDERSTANDS your ups and downs, and allows you "bad days."

LOVE DOESN'T

UNDERMINE your confidence in yourself.

USE you for its own purposes and then discard you.

VENTILATE its emotions on you as a garbage dump.

WRITE YOU OFF because you didn't meet its demands.

LIE for convenience.

REMAIN self-centered.

PROMOTE inflexibility.

ANTICIPATE perfection.

CHAPTER 4

Responsibility...
a detachable burden easily shifted
to the shoulders of God, Fate,
Fortune, Luck or one's neighbor.
In the days of astrology, it was
customary to unload it
upon a star.

- Ambrose Bierce, The Devil's Dictionary 1911

WHO IS RESPONSIBLE FOR THE WAY I FEEL?

Many of my clients have told me when experiencing difficulties in their relationship that they remember being in satisfying relationships previously – but didn't realize it until they were no longer in them. Unfortunately, many people misunderstand the mistakes that were made in those previous relationships and simply consider the marriage or relationship a failed one as though neither party had a great deal of responsibility in it.

Responsibility ownership can be a significant problem in nearly any relationship. We train ourselves, early on, to work harder on other aspects of our lives, and we assume that once married or committed, our relationship will just continue to improve.

When individuals relate to feeling depressed, feeling angry, upset, anxious, irritated, or rejected, they usually focus on external situations – events, people, things, and so on – as the source of those feelings. Unfortunately, as these feelings continue and the emotional and behavioral effects continue, the person can feel helpless with a lack of awareness and insight as to how to resolve the discomfort. The feelings continue without resolution. As a result of a lack of responsibility ownership, the individual will fail to accept that although these situations…or persons…or things…or events…may influence their feelings, they themselves are 100% responsible for not only the creation but the maintenance of those feelings. Although we are certainly influenced by other situations or people, the emotional upsetness we feel comes from our private critic and the voice that we have in our heads that insists external things are upsetting or devaluative. Unfortunately, most of the time, those internal statements are never challenged but just accepted and so the feelings are self-perpetuated. If we could demand proof to substantiate those statements we make, we would be hard-put to come up with the evidence to support them, and it might, in turn, alleviate much of the toxic information that we are feeding ourselves.

In other words, individuals "do depression," "do anxiety," "do worry," "do anger," "do irritation," and so on, by creating a variety of statements that reinforce the feeling. Statements such as, "I never have anything fun to do," "I don't get along with my children," "I'm not a good mother/father," "My partner and I have a poor relationship," "I never have good relationships," "I'm not happy with my job," and, "Why does this always happen to me?" usually result in the generation of not only unhappiness but a persistent sense of unease. This generalized feeling of depression stems from focusing on the feeling of being depressed and never on the actual statements that create the depression.

If we could expend more energy dealing with the alternatives to resolve those negative statements, those feelings of depression would certainly be alleviated and often eliminated. Imagine a pin cushion chock full of pins with little flags and statements on each one that an individual selects, again and again, to emotionally poke themselves, resulting in those bad feelings. The object of responsibility ownership is to get rid of each pin in the pin cushion – one by one – and even replace it...maybe with a box of feathers? Replacing negative messages or personally devaluative statements with affirming thoughts still gets our attention. And it doesn't have to hurt.

Another example of feeling responsibility ownership could be someone saying, "I feel like a kangaroo. Sometimes I hop around. I have a bit of a pouch after eating a meal, and sometimes I wear fuzzy clothes. Would you therefore accept the fact that I am a kangaroo?" As a rule, most people would logically reply, "No, you're not a kangaroo." If then asked to identify why they believe he is not a kangaroo, they might be expected to respond with something like, "Well, kangaroos have long tails, and it's obvious that you don't;" "Kangaroos are covered with fur and it's clear that you aren't;" "Kangaroos do not communicate using human language;" or, "Kangaroos live in the wild and you live in domestic surroundings."

Our subject might still argue, "But I feel like a kangaroo!" Fair enough, however, feeling like a kangaroo does not make a man a kangaroo. If feelings became truth, then – just because we felt them deeply – indeed a person could become a kangaroo.

One person might say to another, "You're a chimpanzee." Must she accept that? One would guess her reply to be a simple, "No, I'm not." If followed with, "Well, you're a rhinoceros then," she again would reply, "Uh no, I'm not." If followed with, "You are inferior, insecure, inadequate or depressed," that same person might suddenly find the words easy to agree with and respond, "Yes, I am."

However, an individual simply saying those things about her doesn't make them true, otherwise she would also be a chimpanzee. Or a rhinoceros. All that the accuser has done is to reinforce something that the individual has continued to say to herself, about herself, in relation to a particular situation or event – one that has made her feel insecure, inferior or depressed. Only in challenging one's private critic can this change. If people would take real responsibility for their own behavior or actions, they would assuredly feel a sense of empowerment. We leave ourselves vulnerable to accepting any negative or devaluative statement that comes our way when we experience those accusations without any documentation or logical support. This is especially true when these statements, for the most part, have been a continuation of the discounting, demeaning or unpleasant statements we've already experienced throughout much of our lives.

You often hear insanity defined as "doing the same thing again and again and expecting different results." Most people have a greater gift for identifying what's wrong with their partner or their relationship than identifying ways to honestly commit to change. They will often seek out and most assuredly find alternatives to meet their needs and justify their unhappiness, rather than exploring the options and opportunities that exist to resolve their impairment and to proactively move in a healthier and more loving direction with each other. Poet, essayist and philosopher Henry David Thoreau once said, "There is no remedy for love but to love more." This is what it takes for individuals to move beyond their anger, resentments, disappointments or unrealistic expectations for their partner. Another poet, Ralph Waldo Emerson, stated, "What lies behind us and what lies before us are tiny matters compared to what lies within us." It is what is within all of us that creates the commitment for change – and so we either commit to a new direction that is positive and loving, or double down in stubbornness to maintain an irrational and unhealthy belief system that prevents us from opening our minds to new thinking and new insight about our partner. In the 1500's Romanian-born Unitarian preacher Francis David stated, "We need not think alike, only to love alike." And that means learning to accept another's differences or belief systems, as long as they don't compromise or devalue us. We must remove ourselves from the archaic, irrational thinking that our relationship must be as we might see portrayed in the movies, on television or in a romance novel. To not subscribe to the fantasy of what could be, but to fully face what is and to work positively from a place rooted firmly in a loving reality.

When connecting with each other initially, things just seemed to click. We explored areas of respect and friendship, shared thoughts and feelings, listened to and had fun with one another. So let's ask ourselves what we did to make that happen. How did we create such enjoyment in connection and love? What do we need to do to revisit that loving connection to each other – the very mortar that we used to lay the bricks of the foundation of our relationship?

CHAPTER 5

A man cannot be comfortable without his own approval.

- Mark Twain, "What is Man?" 1906

THE GOOD LIFE: A MATTER OF CHOICE

WHY CAN'T I FEEL MORE WORTHWHILE?

Individuals in our society appear to be continually rewarding themselves and others for performing and doing. Is this at the expense of thinking and being? I believe so. Sometimes an individual's true worth is minimized and replaced by a person's ability to be "successful" or to perform well in whatever they're doing, and that becomes how we measure their worth. In truth, an individual should not have to rely on an external reason to feel worthwhile. We exist: that fact is reason enough.

A person's warmth, sensitivity, compassion, sincerity, kindness, understanding, affection, and generosity – these are character traits representing, in their truest form, an individual's essence and real self throughout his or her existence. We create a more emotionally healthy perception of our worth, as people, by expending energy in those character areas and then developing them to enhance our lives. Through them you can then perceive yourself and the universe as emotionally wonderful.

However, an individual who gets a raise or a high grade in a class and feels worthwhile may distort his barometer for worthwhileness, just as does an individual who did not get a raise or a passing grade may feel useless. It should be rewarding to one's self to accomplish a particular task or goal, but one's sense of personal importance should not be based in doing so.

When we find ourselves giving up our power in various situations, giving it to someone else because of a particular grade or a particular raise, it can create a perception of insignificance or uselessness. It is a common tendency to compare ourselves to others and come out second-best, which just reinforces our feelings of inferiority.

Let's pull back here. Everyone, in his or her own way, must identify what is most important to them as individuals in their own lives. For example, we all know that eventually we're going to die. The dying part isn't really as important, or as interesting, as the quality of life we experience along the way. Is it things or accomplishments that create one's positive feeling of self until one dies *or* is it the quality we receive in caring and sharing, in kindness, warmth, sensitivity, loyalty, honesty, love, compassion, affection, and a positive emotional connection to others? Each person has a responsibility to ascertain where they assign the greatest awareness – to things and accomplishments outside themselves, or to values of love? That does not mean things, such as personal or work accomplishments, social activities, or the acquisition of objects, don't create a sense of pleasure and happiness. They do. But are they equal on the scale of determining what you find most important? Or where the majority of your energy should go? What do you wish to explore, to cultivate – and ultimately, grow from – as you move forward on life's path? That's the litmus test. As Henry David Thoreau once said,

"The price of anything is the amount of human life you wish to exchange for it."

When people are young they sometimes see themselves as immortal. A youth understands that people get old and eventually die, but from where they sit, death is a long way away. It's far down the timeline, so why waste time thinking about it? At this stage in life people may focus more on quantity than quality – perceiving what they have and do now as most important, maybe skipping over how some experiences are more fulfilling than others. How you can be with someone and still be lonely isn't really top of mind at this stage

THE GOOD LIFE: A MATTER OF CHOICE

because having a relationship is, in and of itself, great. Yet, determining how actions or relationships give life quality is key. When these considerations aren't in the forefront, we then tend to allow individuals or situations to be upsetting to us and create for ourselves a variety of unhealthy behaviors such as worry, depression, anxiety, irrational fears, and so on – which only decrease our quality of life and cause us to make poor trades of our day. And yes, every day we experience a trade of that day. Whether it's a good trade – enjoying the day, enjoying ourselves and how we handled a particular situation; or a bad trade, feeling we wasted so much of it – we will never be able to re-live the day again. As Heraclitus, a great philosopher in 349 B.C., said, "You can never step in the same river twice." Once this day is gone, it is gone. But the advantage we do have is to learn from each day. To learn what we did or did not do that caused us not to experience a good trade, and to actively commit to ourselves that we will make the changes necessary to not repeat the performance, is a choice.

Although each of us has the ability to make changes in every moment, right here and now, it's easy to fall into thinking that we have such a long period of time ahead of us that if we don't do it now, we have plenty of opportunities to do so in the future. As we age, however, we soon realize that the only thing we really do have to show for our life is quality, not quantity. When you pull back and consider things through the filter of all human history, we are on this planet for an infinitesimal time, but we delude ourselves into thinking that we have an abundance of hours and years to straighten out our relationships, or to improve our health habits or any other situations that may be impairing a healthy functioning self. Putting off the changes we know we need to make is one more way we miss the opportunity to establish better trades of our days.

Another message we hear throughout our lives that is expressed both verbally and nonverbally is, "Work hard to be worthwhile."

Obviously, children do not come into the world with this innate belief. But if they perceive significant others in their lives to be highly performance oriented, they may begin to make the choice that the harder they work the better person they will be. This can be reinforced by statements early in life such as, "Those grades are good, but with a little more work you can bring the B up to an A," or "There's always room for improvement," or even, "Idle hands are the devil's workshop." Conditional responses and a lack of positive statements or behavior from the important people in a young person's life become sad proof that if you work harder at something in a particular area, you may gain more acceptance from someone you care about. This can later carry over into one's professional life and be seen in an individual who repeatedly chooses to take on more work to please their employer or to be more accepted by their peers by putting in late hours and allowing others to leave on time. Or by taking the work home and having it consume much of their personal time, thereby creating a handicap for the individual to maintain any type of healthy balance in their life. This can also be seen in the individual who goes on to college and works excessive hours in a part time job, assuming productive responsibilities that maintain a strong work ethic, but leaving little time for a game or a movie or joining friends for pizza. Having a strong work ethic can certainly be an important part of an enjoyable life – but not without a healthy balance.

These individuals may keep themselves extremely productive from the minute they rise in the morning until they collapse into bed late at night, choosing to spend all of their nonemployment-related time doing work around their homes especially in the evenings or on the weekends. And then when they finally are able to carve out some quality and relaxation time, they are too tired or too angry to enjoy it – whether with someone else or especially with themselves.

However, the good news is that behaviors like these – which have

THE GOOD LIFE: A MATTER OF CHOICE

resulted from chronic behavioral reinforcement – can be challenged at any time, and new choices can be made in an effort to establish yourself as a priority, with balance in your life as the ultimate goal. A balanced life will not only enable a person to enjoy a higher energy level, but an energy level of far greater quality, allowing him or her to shine in whatever area of involvement they are associated, or with whomever they are connected. Without such a challenge, they will likely continue to exhibit those same behaviors that will defeat them.

Most of us would like nothing more than to succeed at whatever our endeavor may be in life and to actualize the best of our potential and abilities. Yet so many of us undermine our own ability to reach these goals throughout our lives. This is the shocking paradox of people steering their own ship: they want direction, they make a choice to pursue, but then when entering rough or unsettled waters, instead of charting a new course, they make the choices to endure the difficulty they find themselves in – no matter how self-defeating it may be. It has been said that "You can't control the wind, but you can direct the sail." This does not mean that we should not always commit to doing the best we can in whatever activities we take on. But in accepting the reality that we're doing the best we can, we shouldn't negate ourselves if we don't live up to all the unrealistic expectations out there. We need to be careful not to base our worth on them or let them diminish the successes we do enjoy.

As so eloquently stated in *Autobiography in Five Short Chapters* by author/actress Portia Nelson (appearing later in this book), we find it's often much easier to attempt to avoid the holes in the sidewalk instead of making the conscious choice to walk down a different street.

In the 1700's, Swiss philosopher and writer Jean-Jacques Rousseau said, "Man is born free and everywhere he is in chains." His concerns were largely social chains with customs and laws and conditioning which can hamper creative intelligence. Our concern is primarily with our negative self-talk, which can block the choices we have available to be the best we can be.

When people encounter difficulties in succeeding in various aspects of life, they tend to overlook completely the responsibilities of their inner decisions that produced the failure. Defenses allow us to rationalize and project the blame of responsibility ownership elsewhere. For example, a student finds a teacher difficult and thinks that the teacher is the reason he's unable to achieve adequate grades; an executive blames insurmountable office politics as the reason for failure to get ahead; an alcoholic or drug addict will blame the environment, bad breaks, their significant other, and so on. What these examples have in common is that they all point outward at the cause for failure to succeed, not at the inner self-talk.

In a clinical setting it becomes more obvious to an individual that they have responsibility in the outcome. They make choices available to create that change. But some will still thwart the benefits psychological counseling holds for them as they may have already been too conditioned to exist with their self-destructive behaviors and are too fearful of what life may be like without them. Sigmund Freud termed this "negative therapeutic reaction" and said that "such persons perversely grew worse in treatment at the very time when all signs pointed to a readiness for marked improvement." So we can see here that it's incumbent on the individual to test their adequacy by taking the risk necessary for change – again and again.

CHAPTER 6

Rejection is an Inside Job.

THE GOOD LIFE: A MATTER OF CHOICE

SO WHAT IF I'M INADEQUATE?

If we had to pick a winner for the statement people tend to repeat to themselves, again and again, resulting in the most negativity out there, it would probably be "I'm not good enough" – not perceiving yourself as measuring up, or fearing that others see you that way.

One way to approach inadequacy is to work at accepting and even enjoying one's inadequacy where you can. An inability to perform certain tasks, being devoid of certain skills, being unable to accomplish certain things – being inadequate is all part of being human. All humans have places where they come up short, where they are fallible and imperfect. Instead of focusing and stewing over one's inadequacy, which is what many individuals do (resulting in a personal devaluation and lack of good choices for self), it is far wiser to simply focus on one's adequacy. Even if it's one percent, it's still adequate!

For example, you can tell yourself, "I am a capable wife/husband. I'm a capable employee. Or tennis player, bicycler, trombonist, host or hostess." Capable is really okay. Adequate is really okay. It doesn't mean that you may not strive to become more accomplished in a particular area or regarding a particular behavior. What's unhealthy and a poor choice is to place unrealistic demands on yourself, in terms of a percentage of competence, in order to accept *any* competence.

If I feel that I must be 90 percent adequate as a tennis player, but I am only 70 percent, I may avoid playing tennis altogether. Even if I do practice harder or take lessons, I run the risk of not enjoying it and may lose having tennis be part of the good life for me, no matter how well I play. I evaluate my game on both a conscious and less than conscious level. If I choose to evaluate myself based on my performance, I may harbor gross feelings of inadequacy and throw in strong feelings of inferiority by comparing myself with the person

I am playing against. If they are more proficient at tennis than I am, and hence more adequate at playing the game, I might think they are somehow a better person than me – instead of simply being better at tennis.

That perspective is a choice. One could choose to accept defeat gracefully and continue to see the game as a worthwhile challenge with plenty of room for improvement. One could say, "I'll get them next time," and be happy they're not at home eating junk food on the couch, inactive and unsocial.

Does it now become apparent that the choices we continuously make about the value of our "self" can actually result in an overall healthy or unhealthy lifestyle? The good life is a matter of choice. What's so empowering is that it's available to each and every one of us, here and now, by accepting responsibility for the choices we make.

I CAN NEVER MEASURE UP, SO WHY TRY?

People who maintain feelings of inferiority find that they experience these feelings when comparing themselves to other people and perceive themselves as not measuring up, or coming out second best. This is often due to negative messages and transactions that have taken place from an individual's earliest recollection. Being compared to another family member or someone outside the family with questions such as, "Why can't you be this?" or, "Why couldn't you do that?" or comparison statements such as "Johnny always does this for his parents," or, "Jane never causes her parents any grief," or judgments such as, "Why don't you know the answer, didn't you study?" can lead to a child's negative self-image.

Various messages may be perceived to mean that an individual is lacking in something and that they're not of the same quality as another person. Hence, not only do they feel devalued around someone else, but they may personally devalue themselves before considering getting involved in any particular activity, whether it be with a group or in a one-on-one situation.

For example, in a marital situation: if a spouse is continually discounted, demeaned, or berated – even if the reason is completely unfounded and the spouse knows it – over a prolonged period of time, the spouse's psyche begins to show the effects of taking in this unhealthy emotional food and it ultimately increases negativistic feelings. The length of time over which this occurs and the berated partner's emotional health will determine the extent to which he or she succumbs, as well as how his or her ability to deal with other people and life situations will be affected. If an individual already possesses self-confidence and self-worth they likely are to deal with the negative activity in a more empowered manner.

That said, no matter how many times a person may direct negativistic behavior toward another person, it is still the responsibility of the individual being berated or demeaned to (1) challenge the message, (2) ascertain the validity of the message, and (3) to discard it if it is not valid or accurate, based on the pathology of the person who's sending it. These are the choices we have available to us. Because negativistic behavior from another person is so insidious, it requires an individual to be constantly challenging that negativism and not giving up their emotional credit card, or power, or worth by succumbing to the distorted perceptions or irrational behavior of someone close to them. Like a regular credit card used for personal spending, you can think of your emotional credit card as how you choose to spend your emotions. No matter how strong an individual may be, if they continue to subject themselves to discounting and demeaning behavior on a regular basis, it will, unquestionably, run up an emotional debt and be woven into the way that individual sees him or herself around others, or how willing he or she may be to take risks in testing that adequacy in various situations.

According to Buddha, the spiritual leader and teacher born six centuries before Christ, "Whatever a hater may do to a hater, or an enemy to an enemy, a wrongly directed mind will do us greater mischief."

Once we begin the adventure of both positive and negative experiences, we begin to form, at an early age, a reaction to those experiences or what I like to allude to as "scripts" we receive from the environments in which we find ourselves. These scripts are "written" primarily at an early age, both positively and negatively, by our family; but our peers, school, religious exposure, other adults, television and the media also form them. These messages can come in all shapes and sizes, statements such as:

"Can't you do anything right?"
"You can be anything you want to be."
"Don't speak unless spoken to."
"I'm so glad you're in my life."
"You're not going out looking like that, are you?"
"You have such a kind heart."
"Can't you see I'm busy?"
"I appreciate that you always take care of your things."
"You can't leave the table until clean your plate."
"Why can't you act like so-and-so?"
"You're always so good at _____."
"You'll be the death of me."

Although this is just a brief sampling of messages in the larger scheme of things, it serves to point out the bombardment of scripting we begin to experience and the choices we start making in response to those scripts at an extremely early age of development. Austrian/American psychologist Dr. Rene Spitz, in his books *No and Yes*, and *The First Year of Life*, alludes to our personality and character constructs already being developed by age five, and that we simply improve, augment or rewrite after that.

The life we live with is constantly influenced by the choices that we make in relation to the experiences we encounter.

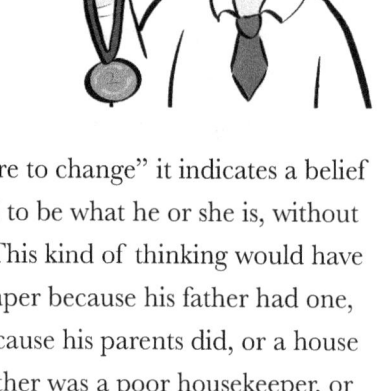

So when you hear people say things such as, "I'm too old to change," or, "That's the way he or she has always been," or, "That's just the way we were raised," or, "He or she doesn't care to change" it indicates a belief that the person is simply destined to be what he or she is, without any opportunity to be different. This kind of thinking would have us believe that a person has a temper because his father had one, or someone drinks excessively because his parents did, or a house is slovenly because a person's mother was a poor housekeeper, or that a person does not pursue an education if no one in his or her family did.

Again, the reality is that the good life *is* a matter of *choice*. We make choices every day to either continue an unhelpful or even destructive pattern of behavior, or make an effort to embrace a sense of empowerment allowing us to change those practices, which have been self-defeating and devaluative to self and others, into something emotionally healthy and supportive. Author Richard Bach, in his book, *Illusions*, said, "There is a test in life to see if your mission is finished. If you're alive, it's not." Certainly the same is true for each of us. Get up every day and embrace life by looking in the mirror and saying, "I really like you, and I'm not going to let anyone or anything interfere with the quality of your day. When you go to bed tonight you will have made another good trade of a day of your life." If we are unable to say this, it's essential that we look for valid evidence to support our unwillingness to accept who we are and do not incorporate a history of negative information without *really* challenging ourselves.

Each and every day that we are alive, we are trading our time for something emotionally healthy and gratifying, or something negative and devaluative. This remains a matter of choice, beginning with our initial decision on how to embrace the day.

Each and every day that we make poor choices which affect the outcome of that trade, it is one more day lost, in whatever length our life may be. When we do arrive at the endpoint of life, unfortunately we cannot look back and have a "do-over" of those days that were wasted or filled with poor choices resulting in negative outcomes. Once the day is spent, it has either been spent for good (healthy) choices or bad (unhealthy) ones.

Let's revisit the private critic discussed earlier. Remember, this critic talks to us on a regular basis, saying things that are positive, uplifting and gratifying, or negative, personally devaluating, demeaning and discounting. For example, the critic might say, "He or she made me so angry." In reality, while a person can influence us, we retain the choice of becoming angry, or accepting an event as disappointing, inconvenient, unpleasant or unacceptable. The choices we make in any given situation or experience can – and do – result in either a healthy or unhealthy physiological response. Hungarian/Canadian endocrinologist Dr. Hans Selye dedicated many years of his career to studying this idea of the psychological made physiological. He's even the one we can credit for first coining the term "stress" in therapeutic circles – we'll learn more about his work in this book's chapter dedicated to the subject. Although no individual can (or should) avoid stress completely, we can employ a variety of techniques to help us deal with its damaging effects in a healthier manner.

The great Greek Stoic philosopher Epictetus stated in 64 A.D., "Men are disturbed only by disturbances in their own minds." This is absolutely true. So, when we experience feelings of rejection, inferiority or defeat – where do they come from? You may need to look no further than your own private critic.

WHY WAIT FOR SOMEONE TO REJECT YOU (WHEN YOU HAVE ALREADY DONE IT YOURSELF)?

From the time we are born, we run the gauntlet through a series of experiences that we have broadly coined as "rejection." And some of us have certainly felt the pangs of rejection far more than others. From our earliest recollection, we have witnessed our parent or parents rejecting us, our siblings rejecting us, our peers rejecting us, and others.

A feeling of rejection can certainly work to reinforce one's negative sense of self, but the problem is that most individuals focus on the emotion and not necessarily the origin of the rejection. The responsibility for rejection is the responsibility of the rejectee, the person feeling rejected, and *not* the rejecter, the person perceived to be doing the rejecting.

A person may say, "I don't like you," or "I don't want to be around you anymore," and one can perceive the statement as, "This is the worst thing that could happen to me," "I am unlovable," "I'm unlikable," "I can't stand the thought of not having this person in my life." Conversely, if one is feeling fairly healthy regarding self, the reaction might instead be something closer to, "I would prefer that this person not leave me, and I would feel better if he or she would discuss their upsetness with me, but I realize that I may not have a choice in the way he or she chooses to do so."

We may have only limited influence on someone else's decision making, but we definitely do have a choice in terms of how we perceive someone else's behavior. Therefore, we might relate that it is a shame or unpleasant or disappointing that someone feels that way or is reacting that way, but it is certainly their loss not having us in their life due to their choices. It is not rejection itself that a person finds upsetting, but the fact that rejection leads to non-love.

If someone rejects someone else, for however long, it becomes apparent that he or she disapproves of them. They may disapprove simply of a behavior or something that the person is not, but it is still perceived as disapproval of the individual and results in non-love, meaning that for a period of time one person is not going to express loving or caring behavior toward the other. Non-love manifests as real abandonment which may last a minute, a day, a week or a lifetime, but in that time one person will abandon the other and no longer be involved with them. This abandonment can, in turn, lead to aloneness and loneliness, some of the most difficult emotional and physical states with which to deal. So, if the individual who feels rejected makes the choice to now see him or herself as unlovable or unlikable or unacceptable, they will usually find this choice reinforced by their feelings of aloneness and the emotion of loneliness.

No one person can reject another unless they're given permission to do so. One of the best ways to deal with rejection is to challenge the behavior or statements of another individual and ascertain the validity of what the person is saying. If this isn't possible and the feelings of loneliness do occur, the best course is to then explore ways of being around people or in situations where they will not feel alone or isolated.

A person might make contact with people whom they know to have positive feelings for them, to help alleviate those feelings of loneliness. That, in turn, will enable them to psychologically begin to challenge the credibility of the discounting, demeaning, verbally and/or emotionally abusive statements that resulted in a state of rejection.

No matter what emotion a person is dealing with, it becomes more profitable and healthy to deal with that emotion from a state of responsibility ownership – knowing that one's choices regarding oneself (or in response to someone else's perceptions and behaviors) ultimately result in either a good life or an emotionally unhealthy one.

We must understand that every person is responsible for his or her own thoughts, actions and behaviors. Each and every one of us has power and control over unhealthy versus healthy perceptions of self, as well as the ability to change any unhealthy perception. The good life is as much about taking risks – emotionally or physically – as it is about gratifying needs. The more risk an individual has committed him or herself to take, the greater the possibility of gratifying their specific needs to create a happier and healthier life.

Let's qualify what we mean by risk here. There's risk involved in asserting yourself, or letting someone know how you feel, and when you're being honest about those feelings someone may become upset or critical with you. Risk may be making your own decisions instead of manipulating someone else to make decisions for you so that you don't have to be wrong and criticized – hence the risk here is exposing yourself to that criticism. An example of this kind of manipulation might be answering the question of "What movie would you like to see?" with an answer of, "I don't care, any movie is fine." Or when "Where would you like to go for dinner?" is answered by, "It doesn't matter to me, I can eat anything." The answerer may be avoiding making a decision that risks the other person being displeased, because if the suggested movie isn't so great or the dinner is of poor quality, it may result in a response of, "That movie was a waste of money," or, "That's the last time I'll ask you where we eat."

Dag Hammarskjold, who served as Secretary General of the United Nations in the 1950's, once said, "An individual who avoids taking risk and plays it safe, is an individual who will live in a world of the utmost insecurity."

As we listen to the words of many great thinkers, it appears that they innately understood the importance of the choices we make and the healthy or unhealthy effects of those choices.

So much of the unhealthiness that we experience in life is due to our perception that we can't change, or in bringing things up from the past to create emotional upsetness in the present.

Once an event has taken place, we cannot go back and change it but we can learn from it and then move ahead. Heraclitus also said, "In changing we find purpose." This speaks to our need to challenge the way we think, and how we react to thoughts about past events, so that we can embrace and enjoy every aspect of life that is available to us and help find the purpose we are seeking.

It is obvious that there are many events that are not within our control – but the choices we make around those events *are* still within our control. This could include health issues, trauma in one's family, or the termination of a relationship. We cannot control that the event is happening but we still are able to choose the way we will accept it.

From the time we're young we hear statements such as, "That makes me upset," "It's because of what someone else said," or, "If he or she wouldn't have done that..." These are the types of statements that encourage us to avoid responsibility ownership for the choices we make and the result is the emotional responses that occur. When we take ownership of the responsibility for our own behavior with the firm concept that "I am responsible for the way I feel, the way I think and the way I behave," we become participative in our ability to make the necessary choices to change the negative experience. Lack of ownership is a behavior pattern that can follow us throughout our lives and may consistently impair a positive resolve to emotional situations. This is especially true in the avoidance of compromise that can be found in the most significant relationships.

As we continue to feel the strength of ownership for our choices – and in challenging the negative statements we say to ourselves *about* ourselves – we begin to experience the good life, each day, in a way that becomes reflexively responsive to the voice of our private critic. We begin to experience it in a way that's healthier, more empowering and ultimately, a more accurate reflection of our life.

CHAPTER 7

The structure of a play is always
the story of how the birds
came home to roost.

- Arthur Miller

THE WORLD IS A STAGE - WHAT PART AM I TRYING OUT FOR?

Challenging our scripts is essential to our ability to ascertain what aspect of our script is healthy and leads to the good life and what aspect of our script is conversely true. Scripts such as, "Work hard to be worthwhile," "Be strong, be perfect," "Don't make waves," "Don't speak unless you're spoken to," "Go over it again and again until you're sure it's right," or, "If you continue to act that way you're going to turn out just like your father (or sister or whomever)" – those scripts go on and on. This is why it's so essential that we challenge the scripts we live with: to ensure that not only are they a good fit for us, but a good fit for those we are responsible to and for. If you wear a size 9 shoe, and are given a size 12, that's an ill fit, but if you wear them long enough you can begin to accommodate the difficulty in that fit and still manage to get around, maybe not even paying much attention to the cumbersome manner in which you do so.

Ill fits can be the result of not owning the responsibility for one's own behavior, and therefore relinquishing control over the outcome. You may blame the earthworm, butterfly, bumblebee, and a thousand others for the plight of your experience, but in reality you need to look inside yourself to see the choices you're making are based on the messages you are receiving from your own internal, private critic.

Almost everyone grows up and experiences life by responding to the emotional stimuli they encounter due to the events around them or statements made by others. The emotional upheaval that one experiences will usually result from the choices he or she is making based on an event. Responses such as, "How dare that person do that to me!" or, "Why does this always have to happen to me?" or, "I always get treated this way," usually result in us poking ourselves with a pin or putting on the "poor me, ain't it awful" label, ultimately leading us into some doom and gloom situation. At the heart of the matter lies the choice we make regarding the event and perhaps not challenging or looking for proof that what we are telling ourselves is really happening. When an individual gets into the emotional state of awful-izing, horrible-izing, terrible-izing and/or catastrophe-izing, he or she ends up…immobile-izing.

If we get into the habit of making a personal commitment each day to like who we are, of making the choice to change those things that we find unacceptable, and personally commit to not allowing anyone or anything to interfere with the quality of our day, by the time we head to bed we will have experienced trading positive energy for positive closure for the day. You hear many people nearing an endpoint in their lives say that if they only had the last twenty years to do over again, they would do things differently. They would not get upset over little things or the way people act or the way certain events occur, because in the larger scheme of things, what's really important is quality of life and how we spent each day embracing our time.

Back in the 1950's, as a medic in Korea, I heard the same statement many times from the person who assisted me in the medical facility. When I would get really upset because I didn't receive the medical supplies I needed in order to treat the personnel I was responsible for, he would look at me with expressive eyes and say, "kwenchana, kwenchana." I responded with the phrase I understood to mean, "I don't understand." He would go on to say, "Look around. People no food.

No place to live, dying. And you complain of needle and thread." What "kwenchana" means is – don't get upset over little things. This was something the Korean people understood very clearly due to four thousand years of conflict they had experienced. (Later, in the West, a very successful book was written by psychotherapist and motivational speaker Richard Carlson entitled, *Don't Sweat the Small Stuff*.) Same idea.

When things are not the way we would like them to be, or do not turn out the way we envision them needing to be, if we could say to ourselves, "kwenchana" (pronounced "kin-shana") and embrace its message, the choice regarding the outcome would be that much healthier and more emotionally satisfying.

Research and stress testing indicate that one of the highest level stressors that we can experience is an impaired relationship with a significant other. How can we avoid difficulty in those important relationships if we incorporate poor choice-making and negative or devaluative statements from our private critic into the way we deal with various aspects of that relationship?

Conversely, research also indicates that there appears to be no greater emotional gratification than successful relationships with significant others.

Life is like health – we often don't truly appreciate it or embrace it until we no longer have it. The adventure we find ourselves experiencing – from the day we're born until we die – varies in time, situations and events, but we do have a choice in terms of how we will challenge outcomes. It is not the *situation* that gives us the most difficulty but the conversation we have with ourselves, and the choices we make pertaining to that conversation, that will ultimately create a positive or negative outcome. Therefore, the more situations we experience that elicit a healthier choice, the better the life. Whatever time each of us has, the good life will always be a matter of choice.

CHAPTER 8

If I don't change my behavior,
I can't change my journey.

THE GOOD LIFE: A MATTER OF CHOICE

BEHAVIOR

To regain the empowerment to change and become the best person you can be, you must give yourself permission, and assert your right to be treated with kindness and respect simply because you exist. It was film director and writer Martin St. Charles who in 1982 said,

I pledge allegiance to all the things that are good about me
and I will from this day forward
no longer try to be everything to everybody,
nor will I be someone I am not.
I will no longer use all of my energies
to fulfill the dreams of others while mine go unattended.
I will use my assertive right to take charge of my life.
I will never again know guilt, for this pain is self-chosen.
I will fight the manipulators and their ploys
by standing up for myself and my ideals.
I will insist on being treated with dignity,
and demand goodness in my life.
I will speak the truth quietly and clearly and listen to others.
I will be the judge of my behavior, thoughts and emotions
and I will be responsible for them.
I will always challenge putdowns.
I will destroy negative thoughts and fears of rejection.
I will not distress myself with imaginings.
I will be gentle with myself and strive to be happy.
I will live positively and I will begin now.

The Buddhist religion holds that the suffering of mankind is produced by attachment to a previous condition of existence. This begs the question, how many of us rewrite our negative scripting, or even believe that it's possible?

We all have a private critic that either embraces our life in a positive way or will say things that are incredibly self-defeating. Like tennis champ John Peers once said, "You can't lead a cavalry if you think that you look funny riding a horse." Two thousand years ago, Marcus Aurelius, who was both a Roman emperor and Stoic philosopher, said, "Our life is what our thoughts make it." And First Lady Eleanor Roosevelt stated, "No one can make you feel inferior without your consent."

Although we have had great insights offered to us by others over the years, in an attempt to encourage us to see life in a healthier manner and live life with the quality that is our right, many of us continue to view change in a cynical fashion. As H.L. Mencken, an American journalist and satirist, said, "A cynic is a man who, when he smells flowers, looks around for a coffin."

It needs to be about the commitment we make each day to be the best we can be. This does not mean we won't make mistakes or fail to achieve certain goals, but that we will expend the energy necessary to attempt to be the best we can be. As French poet and politician Louis, marquis de Fontanes, said in the 1700's, "The desire for perfection is the worst disease that ever afflicted the human mind." When we allow ourselves to believe that there can always be some sort of positive result – no matter what the occurrence – we'll always know what the nature of the outcome is, and we will gain the inner strength to test our adequacy in other directions. It is reminiscent of an old Zen saying, "My barn having burned to the ground, I can now see the moon."

The question we all must ask ourselves is, "Who are we, really? Are we the person we feel we should be or could be or ought to be?

Or a person who plays a role – although a poor fit emotionally – to avoid any potential conflict or dissatisfaction from others?" We've often heard quoted English playwright William Shakespeare who reminds us, "All the world's a stage." Are we living genuinely or playing at who we want people to think we are?

In the cartoon, *Potshots*, two people are speaking and one says to the other, "Why do you take life so seriously? We won't get out of it alive anyway!" This is true for all of us. If we could find more laughter, more humor, more happiness and enjoyment in what we do each day, we'd benefit from an inexpensive and natural medicine that could help our bodies and minds function in a healthier way.

Research shows that laughter has a positive influence on our human organ systems, yet we continue the cycle of going to our local pharmacy and purchasing over-the-counter aids to address our different symptoms – many of which might be alleviated or even eliminated by changing our thinking, our sense of empowerment and our personal commitment to self.

People will feel down or "do" depression, which is usually based on their private conversations with self regarding situations or events that have not occurred in the way they would have liked, or the comparisons they make of themselves to other people or situations. Just like the 'Poor Me: Ain't it Awful?' and other 'Doom and Gloom' kinds of thoughts we have regarding that private conversation, we have the ability to challenge that negativistic thinking and replace it with healthier choices. This is best done by looking at all of the positives that do exist for us, instead of focusing on the downside of life that is full of things that don't always occur the way we would like.

Worry is another thief that steals the opportunity of making good choices because we cannot be worried and, at the same time, be fulfilling our agreement with ourselves that we won't allow someone or something else to interfere with the quality of our day. Worry may act as an unconscious superstition we use, believing that if we worry about something, it most likely won't occur. But we should ask ourselves, "How many worries throughout our lives have ever come true or have even come close?"

The answer is probably very few. The illogical aspect of worry is that no matter what we may obsess about in a negativistic or fatalistic manner, that thing is either going to happen or not happen – whether we worry about it or not. In the meantime, how much opportunity for positive thinking in our lives is being consumed instead by negativistic thinking? As American humorist Erma Bombeck said, "Worry is like a rocking chair: It gives you something to do, but it doesn't get you anywhere."

Remember, reality is based on a frame of reference. How do we perceive life around us? At best, in many ways, reality is often pretty ambiguous, leaving it open to our own interpretation. For example, two priests are talking and one asks the other, "Is it all right if I smoke when I pray?" The other priest responds, "No!" The first priest then asks, "Is it all right if I pray when I smoke?" and the second priest replies, "Sure! Prayer is good with any activity." See what I mean?

CHAPTER 9

Risk taking is essential for change.

RISK

Life is all about taking risks and gratifying needs. The more risks we take, the more confidence we gain and the better our self-esteem and self-concept. There are things that you enjoy every day which seemed risky when you first attempted them.

We often create imaginary horror when we talk to ourselves about the irrational consequences of risk, whether it be fear of being rejected, of experiencing a new place, of speaking in front of people, and the list goes on and on.

Stop debating it. Let's take a chance and do it. No matter how anxious we may feel based on the negative messages of our private critic, we should do it – as long as the situation is not a violation of our person or a threat to our survival. Failure comes when fear causes avoidance of testing our adequacy or taking the risk. We have a tendency to put self-defeating labels on events when we fear they won't work out, such as, "I'll be worthless, I'll be incompetent, I'll be far less than those around me," instead of challenging that stream of negativity. You are fallible. You are imperfect. You are human.

Life is predicated on risk and knowing that we don't always achieve the desired outcome. But, we grow from our setbacks – and so the risk is worth the potential reward.

In risk-taking, so many individuals fear rejection by others, which prevents them from challenging their fear and testing their adequacy. Rejection may not be what they will experience, but that fear of rejection can be overwhelming. As we discussed earlier, rejection leads to disapproval, which then leads to non-love, leading to abandonment, and ultimately, aloneness and loneliness. Wow, that's pretty heavy. But again, that loneliness is often reinforced by playing 'Poor Me, Ain't it Awful' and 'Doom and Gloom,' instead of taking the risk to be around another person or people who will acknowledge you or show you kindness or respond to your psychological needs.

Most people reward themselves for performing and doing, not thinking and being. Anytime they must do something they're not familiar with, one in which they lack confidence, it reinforces their fear of not performing well – instead of stimulating emotional growth by allowing them to try something new, even though the confidence isn't there yet. Sometimes it helps to sit down, close your eyes and create an image of taking those risks and succeeding. If you do not attain that success either in thought or reality, ask yourself: What's the worst thing that could happen if all this doesn't go the way I would like it to? Most of us end up awful-izing, horrible-izing, terrible-izing, catastrophe-izing, ultimately immobilizing ourselves with what could happen, instead of acknowledging that it may simply be disappointing or somewhat unpleasant or uncomfortable – mostly a pain in the posterior. Those are things you can pretty easily deal with, even if you don't like them.

If someone responds to a situation with unpleasant or unacceptable feelings, they will usually say, "He/She/That made me upset and made me feel bad." But if other people truly had that much influence, it would make just as much sense for them to tell you, "You're a bear," and have you accept it. Instead you simply counter, "I don't look like a bear, I don't have fur like a bear and I don't have the genetic makeup of a bear." By ascertaining immediately that you are not indeed a bear, you allow yourself to dismiss such a statement as ridiculous.

This is no different than what you need to do when someone says something hurtful. You must quietly challenge it in the same way and be consciously aware of the challenging. Remember, just because someone said something doesn't make it true. It is what *you* say to yourself *about* yourself in relation to what others say that confirms any of the negativity they might send your way.

THE GOOD LIFE: A MATTER OF CHOICE

English writer Christopher Logue wrote a poem titled, "Come to the Edge," which reads:

"Come to the edge." he said.
"We can't. We're afraid." they said.
"Come to the edge." he said.
"We can't. We will fall!"
"Come to the edge."
And they came.
And he pushed them.
And they flew.

To look at this in a different way, I turn to popular author Portia Nelson, from a book entitled, *There's a Hole in My Sidewalk*.

Autobiography in Five Short Chapters:

Chapter 1
I walk down the street.
There is a deep hole in the sidewalk.
I fall in.
I am lost...I am helpless.
It isn't my fault.
It takes forever to find a way out.

Chapter 2
I walk down the same street.
There is a deep hole in the sidewalk.
I pretend I don't see it.
I fall in again.
I can't believe I am in the same place.

But it isn't my fault.
It still takes a long time to get out.

Chapter 3
I walk down the same street.
There is a deep hole in the sidewalk.
I see it is there.
I still fall in...it's a habit.
My eyes are open.
I know where I am.
It is my fault.
I get out immediately.

Chapter 4
I walk down the same street.
There is a deep hole in the sidewalk.
I walk around it.

Chapter 5
I walk down another street.

It's not important how long we have been thinking or experiencing life in an unhealthy way; what is important is that we challenge ourselves to walk down a different street. People say, "I'm too old to change," or, "I've been doing this for too long." But, like baseball pitcher Satchel Paige said, "How old would you be if you didn't know how old you are?" And Billie Burke, screen star from the film *The Wizard of Oz*, once said, "Age is of no importance unless you are a cheese."

THE GOOD LIFE: A MATTER OF CHOICE

The key has nothing to do with how old we are or how much time we may have. It's whether or not we are willing to make a personal commitment to be the best we can be with the time we do have. In order to take steps in a more positive, emotionally gratifying direction, we must be willing to challenge our fears, test our adequacy and take on those risks that will genuinely enhance the quality of our total being.

Most people who are fearful of taking risks won't allow themselves to make mistakes due to past scripts and perceived negative responses from others. More powerful are the negative perceptions of self that stem from denying our own humanness and refusing to admit that we are fallible and imperfect. Like advertising executive Leo Burnett said, "To swear off making mistakes is very easy. All you have to do is swear off having ideas."

You have the right to be who you are and who you want to be, as long as it doesn't compromise anyone else. You have the right to grow and to change and to reach any particular goal limited only by your ability or talent. You have the right to love and be loved and accepted and cared for although you cannot control the responses of others. You have the right to self-respect and the enhancement of your self-concept and self-esteem as long as you're not hurting anyone else in the process.

We all have the right to be happy and to find those things in the world that are meaningful and rewarding and give us a sense of completeness, gratification and stability. We have the right to live the way we choose – to continue living the way we are, or to change that way at any given time with the goal of having to have a better life. And we have the right to enforce the changes we need to make that enable us to do so.

STAYING ANGRY IS ALLOWING SOMEONE TO LIVE RENT-FREE IN YOUR MIND

Anger is the emotional state we find ourselves in when we cannot accept or tolerate the humanness of others or ourselves – when something has been done that we don't believe should have been done. Anger also happens when we cannot tolerate something coming out differently than how it was "supposed to," often as a result of expectations that were unrealistic to begin with. Psychiatrist Frederick Perls said in his Gestalt prayer, "I am not in this world to live up to your expectations, and you are not in this world to live up to mine. You are you and I am I, and if by chance we find each other, then it is beautiful. If not, it can't be helped."

Any time you allow someone to influence you, creating anger, or when you create anger in yourself over an event or a situation, you're allowing someone or something to live rent-free in your mind in an emotionally unsettling way. Certainly, irrational thinking is nothing new and irrational beliefs have occurred since the beginning of time. In fact, there have been different philosophers throughout the ages who have addressed the issue of anger or emotional disruption. In 64 A.D., the philosopher Epictetus advised, "If you do not wish to be prone to anger, do not feed the habit; give it nothing which may tend to its increase." And Emperor Marcus Aurelius said, "Our life is what our thoughts make it."

An old Cherokee chief tells us, in speaking to his grandson about the battle that goes on inside people, "My son, the battle is between two wolves inside us all. One is Evil. It is anger, envy, jealousy, sorrow, regret, greed, arrogance, self-pity, guilt, resentment, inferiority, lies, false pride, superiority, and ego. The other is Good. It is joy, peace, love, hope, serenity, humility, kindness, benevolence, empathy, generosity, truth, compassion and faith." The grandson thinks about it for a minute and then asks his grandfather, "Which wolf wins?" The old Cherokee man simply replies, "The one you feed."

And as liberal minister Harry Emerson Fosdyk once stated, "Hating people is like burning down your house to get rid of a rat."

We all have to ask ourselves, what positive or productive activity occurs by "doing anger" or "doing hatred" toward somebody else? It simply yields poor feelings. Instead it would appear to be more productive to maintain an assertive posture and let someone know in a respectful fashion that their behavior or statements or attitude are unacceptable. That doesn't mean that if you feel the need to tell someone to stop doing or saying something, you can't say "stop." You certainly can. And if you need to tell someone "no," say "no." But whatever the words you choose, you can share those feelings in a respectful way that still allows you to respond with empowerment and to embrace the situation in a healthier manner.

CHAPTER 10

*I find my joy of living
in the fierce and ruthless battles of life
and my pleasure comes
from learning something.*

- Auguste Strindberg
Miss Julie, 1888

THE GOOD LIFE: A MATTER OF CHOICE

STRESS

Stress has been a part of human existence since the days when cavemen first roamed the earth. But we didn't really begin to understand its damaging effects on our own bodies until about the 1900's. One could assume that early humans experienced significant stress on a regular basis – through fight or flight perils, struggles against the elements or the basic search for food – and those kinds of experiences have continued, in some fashion, throughout our history.

So, what is stress? It's a state of mental or emotional strain resulting from adverse or demanding circumstances. We can all agree that life is challenging, given the demands we place on ourselves in maintaining some modicum of success in our daily lives – whether it be at work, in parenting, in relationships, or even on a golf course, giving our emotional credit card to that little white ball. Many stressors are also increased in our wired world, where people live with a cell phone in their pocket or continuously on their ear – talking or texting, or alternately, focusing on a computer or tablet. For most of us, there are hundreds of other demands already in place. The question that needs to be raised is, " how do these stressors, and the emotional/physical responses they generate, support the balance that we need in life to recharge our emotional and physiological batteries?"

In early 1900's psychology, the James-Lang Theory suggested that we experienced sadness because we wept. A few years later, the Cannon-Bard Theory disputed that concept, stating that we are not sad because we are weeping, we weep because we are sad. Remember, it bears repeating that although this seemed to be great insight into our emotional makeup, it was much earlier – around two thousand years before – that Greek philosopher Epictetus told us that, "people are not disturbed by things but by the view which they take of them."

And he further reflected that, "people are disturbed only by disturbances in their own minds." He understood that our private critic and our thoughts are forever influenced by to the experiences around us and lead us to respond in a healthy or unhealthy manner.

It has been found that when an individual experiences stressful situations, there are significant outputs of chemicals like adrenaline, norepinephrine, adrenocorticotropic hormones, and cortisol, which can influence the organ systems in a negative manner. Research also shows that under prolonged or chronic stress, the weakest organ system can be particularly vulnerable. Even the T lymphocytes are affected in one's immune system. For example, a low level of T lymphocytes can be found six to eight weeks into bereavement after the loss of a significant other. This depletion of T lymphocyte levels in our bodies can lead to a significantly compromised immune system and leave us exposed to a whole host of ailments.

Findings further reinforce the significant impact stress can have on people in impaired relationships. Not working to improve an unsound relationship furthers the potentially damaging effects on health. In other studies, research has shown that in cancer-prone rats, those enclosed in an environment with an irritating, noxious electrical charge have an over 80 percent higher rate of cancer. However, those in the same environment that are allowed to step on a bar to control that noxious charge experience only a 10 to 15 percent higher rate of cancer. And ulcer-prone monkeys that are separated from their mothers prematurely experience much higher incidences of ulcers as compared to those separated in a normal maturation period.

But again, it's not the amount of stress that you have, it's how you respond to it. Remember me mentioning endocrinologist Hans Selye earlier in the book? In the 1950's, he coined the word "stress" in stating his theory of the General Adaption Syndrome of alarm, resistance and exhaustion, which promotes physiological changes that can have damaging effects on the human organ system. And, thirty years later, in his article in "Executive Health" in February, 1983, Dr. Selye stated that no concept related to human health and function had been more commonly talked about for so many years than what we term "stress."

Stress is linked to diseases such as arthritis, ulcers, kidney disease, heart disease, circulatory disturbances, and so many other problems, according to Dr. Selye, but he did not actually conclude that stress was the cause. Instead, it's the *reaction* to the stress — when the reaction is *distress*, physiological problems are often caused.

Stress then, according to Dr. Selye, can actually be the spice of life. It's associated with all types of activity, and therefore may only be avoided by doing nothing, which doesn't sound like much of a life. So distress, or what we call stress, depends not on what happens to an individual but upon the way he or she *reacts*.

Stress can certainly cause you to break down. But remember, it can also bring great satisfaction. Dr. Selye spent a lifetime studying these contrasting ideas. For the majority of his career, he was professor and director of the Institute of Experimental Medicine and Surgery at the University of Montreal. Prior to this he trained at the University of Prague, the University of Paris, and the University of Rome. He received both a medical degree and a doctorate in chemistry in 1931, and ultimately ended up at McGill University in Montreal. Through all his work on the subject, he postulated that there are three sets of changes a person experiences when exposed to stress of a significant degree.

An individual first goes into Alarm Reaction, where the body experiences a call to arms or defensive measures. This is Phase 1 of the General Adaptation Syndrome. Physiologically speaking, Cortisol and DHEA hormones are elevated. The adrenal cortex enlarges while other lymphatic structures shrink. Bleeding ulcers may appear in the stomach and the upper gut of some individuals. Tissue breakdown, low blood glucose levels, and insomnia are all common too. If exposure to the noxious situation continues, the Phase 2 State of Adaption or Resistance follows. Low blood sugar levels and trouble sleeping may also continue. Ultimately, Phase 3 is the State of Exhaustion. In this last phase, the body loses the ability to adapt, burnt out from stress. Now, Cortisol, DHEA, and Epinephrine are all low. Typical symptoms may include severe fatigue, allergies, the same inability to sleep through the night, and salt cravings.

Selye observed that many elements, including various emotional disturbances, mild headaches, insomnia, upset stomach, sinus attacks, high blood pressure, ulcers, rheumatic or allergic afflictions as well as heart, blood vessel, and kidney diseases, are stirred up and encouraged by the body itself due to faulty adaptive reaction in that second stage.

So why is it that the same stressor can cause such different afflictions in one person as opposed to another? That's where conditioning factors bcome in. They may include someone's genetic predisposition, age, sex, and a host of other influencers including the scripting an individual has developed over time in order to deal with various stressors.

Say you're at a party and are talking with someone who has been drinking excessively. If that person hurls an insult at you, nothing will likely happen if you simply choose to move on and talk to someone else. But if you respond by verbally fighting, or even by preparing to do so, you discharge hormones and increase your blood pressure and pulse rate. With that response, your whole nervous system will become alarmed and tense in anticipation of combat. This ends up being physically self-destructive and in prolonged and chronic stress, the weakest organ system can be affected as discussed earlier.

Whenever a negative, upsetting situation is experienced, an individual has two ways to handle it. Either he or she can go around feeling victimized and distressed, or move on, and get as much out of the rest of the day as they possibly can.

In an example from Dr. Selye, the mother who is told that her only son died in battle suffers a terrible mental shock, but if years later it turns out that the news was false and the son unexpectedly walks into the room alive and well, she experiences extreme joy. The specific results of the two events, sorrow and joy, are completely different, in fact opposite to one another. Yet their stressor effect – the nonspecific demand to readjust to an entirely new situation – may be the same.

Dr. Selye felt that some of the more effective ways to deal with the incident of negative stress are to build resistance by regular sleep, exercise and good health habits, to compartmentalize work and non-working life, to talk things through with someone who may act as a support system, and to withdraw physically from the stress-inducing situation, if possible.

He also postulated that the most important goal of a person is not to work as little as possible, but to find an occupation which feels more like play than work. We know now from research that individuals who, later in life, maintain purpose and are gratified by such, seem to have fewer incidents of problems, especially thought disorders.

I'm sure Dr. Selye would agree that the primary goal in life would be making good trades every day that reduce the damaging effects of the stressors you encounter.

In his paper, "Modulation of Host Defenses by Personality in Stress," University of Colorado medical researcher John Cohen, in collaboration with psychiatrist Linda Crnic and behavioral geneticist Linda Dixon, reported that, "In animals, stress is clearly immune suppressive and mimics the effects of cortical steroid treatment; this strengthens the view that stress operates primarily via the hypothalamic-pituitary adrenal cortical axis."

The experiments demonstrate a direct correlation between an animal's behavior or personality and the set level of its immune response. Dr. Cohen reported that stress has been shown to depress certain functions of the immune system. For example, recall that people whose spouses have died have decreased T lymphocyte function in their blood for at least six weeks after bereavement. Such people also have a higher than expected death rate due in part to an increased frequency of infections, autoimmune disease and cancer. Other studies of long-term life stress also suggest a relation to illness. In the Social Readjustment Rating Scale (SRRS), also known as the Holmes and Rahe Stress Scale, life changes are assigned points based on how stressful they are and the frequency of illness correlates with the number of points accumulated.

At the Albert Einstein College of Medicine in New York City, two groups of rat pups were experimented with, regarding the normal predisposition of ulcers. They prematurely separated the experimental group at 14 days and later tested both the experimental and control group who had both been deprived of food. With the group that had been prematurely separated, between 80 and 90 percent of their group numbers had ulcers, where only 10 to 20 percent of the control group that were separated at the normal time of 21 days, had ulcers.

In short, more distress equals more pain.

In August and September of 1985, a large U.S telephone survey was made of persons representing a cross-section of adults, and the results were published in the *Nuprin Pain Report Survey*. In the survey people who said they experienced stress everyday were labeled "the high stress group," and those who reported less stress were labeled "the low stress group." When comparing the groups several differences emerged. In each of the seven categories of pain used in the study (headache, backache, muscle, joint, stomach, menstrual, and dental), the high stress group was more likely to be at least an occasional victim. In the previous year, 14 percent of the high stress group had experienced 101 or more days of headaches. The low stress group? Just 2 percent. Also in the previous year 20 percent of the high stress group had reported more than 100 days of backaches, compared with only 7 percent of the low stress group.

When we talk about stress, we are talking about the negative reactions. For some it may be a headache or an achy back while for others it may result in even more serious concerns.

Dr. Donald Tubesing, a psychologist from Duluth, Minnesota, and author of *Kicking Your Stress Habits*, likens stress to the tension on a violin string: "You need enough tension to make music, but not so much that it snaps."

Although there are many ways to manage the various stressors you experience, one of the most immediate and successful ways of reducing negative stress is in experiencing empowerment over your negative private critic.

Dr. Peter Angerer, an aptly-named professor and physician at the University of Munich, studied 150 patients with coronary heart disease and in a report in the Journal of American College of Cardiology, those 150 patients answered questions in a self-report questionnaire concerning emotional support, anger suppression and hostility. What Dr. Angerer found was that the people who reported to have high levels of expressed anger and low levels of social support were much more likely to develop cardiovascular disease.

Now, again, not all stress is "bad stress" or stress that is harmful to an individual. There's a lot we do every day that is good stress, like going to work, taking care of a home, schlepping kids from one place to the other, getting groceries, playing sports, and so on. Healthy or manageable stress can be determined as such by gauging whether or not it gratifies our needs and results in our making a good trade of that day – or if it is interfering with making that good trade.

In addition to that Nuprin list, symptoms that indicate too much stress include (take a deep breath here): dry mouth, headache, sighing, overeating/undereating, chain smoking, stomach cramps, diarrhea/constipation, nausea, feeling "faint," stroking, pulling or twirling hair, clenched fists, nervous cough, mouth noises (such as tongue clucking), talking too much/too fast, inability to talk, "lump" in throat, lack of sexual interest, sweating, menstrual irregularities, blushing, fingernail biting, leg wagging, rocking back and forth, depression, irritability/anger/resentment, tic in the eye or elsewhere, desire to "run away," muscle spasms/tightness, fatigue/weariness, boredom, hypochondria, clammy hands, lip biting, ready tears, hyperactivity/listlessness, inability to be alone, sleeping issues, heart palpitations, distractibility, proneness to errors, decreased productivity, confusion, alcohol/drug dependence, nightmares, butterflies in the stomach, excessive giggling, ulcers, indigestion and skin problems. That's one long list!

Self-talk that can be stressful is found in all sorts of statements like, "When people do not accept me or disapprove of me it means that I am unacceptable or bad," "My worth may depend on how much I may produce or achieve or the income I make," "I must go to great lengths to please others or they will not like me and may abandon or reject me," "It's horrible when things don't go the way I want them to or when people don't act the way I would like them to act," or, "I must be perfect and competent in everything I attempt to do." And coming in at number one on German psychoanalyst Karen Horney's List of the Ten Most Neurotic needs is, "It's critical to have love and approval from everyone all the time."

It would be far more helpful to say the following things to yourself instead: "If I'm not happy with the way I feel or act, I need to look at the way I'm thinking or behaving and challenge my private critic to see whether my thinking is realistic or valid. Might I be exaggerating

THE GOOD LIFE: A MATTER OF CHOICE

those particular thoughts?" I need to understand that my thinking and what I'm saying *to* myself *about* myself directly affects the way I feel. This means, if I don't like the way I am feeling I should look at the way I am thinking – further underscoring the idea that the good life is attainable by me and *is* a matter of choice.

Dr. Jerry's Rules for Reducing Stress in Your Life:

- Affirm yourself. Challenge your external negativity. See yourself in a positive light.

- Put things in their places. Organization can be relaxing.

- Live in the present. Set goals for the future. Understand the past.

- Be in control of your private critic, the little voice in your head, and challenge the validity of what you are thinking.

- Try not to escalate problems with "always" and "never" statements. Don't awful-ize, terrible-ize, horrible-ize, catastrophe-ize or, ultimately, immobilize.

- Make sure that each day you do something just for you and, at the end of the day, make sure it was a good trade of your day. Give yourself time for pleasure.

- Compartmentalize whenever possible. Prioritize and don't stack one thing on top of another, which not only creates more anxiety, but overwhelms and immobilizes.

- Learn that "No." is a complete sentence. Most people want to please others all the time and if they say, "No," they feel guilty and have to explain themselves. Remember: you always maintain the right to simply say "No" when appropriate.

- Don't waste your energy trying to be perfect. Be who you are. We're all human, fallible and imperfect. Don't sweat the small stuff.

- Plan dates with your friends, spouse, and others close to you. Write them in your schedule and keep them.

- Schedule your time appropriately. Don't try to fit too much in, or double book yourself.

- Stop trying to always be "first." Go for the silver sometimes.

- Remember that sometimes things just heal themselves and that you don't have to fix everything. It's okay not to do everything.

- If something in your physical environment doesn't work, fix it or get it replaced rather than let it annoy you.

- Try not to own other people's problems. Realize they are responsible for their own actions and behavior. Rescuers usually end up victims.

- Get a handle on your finances. Develop a spending plan.

- Reframe. Think of issues as challenges rather than problems.

- Stop "shoulding" yourself and focus on "wanting to."

- Try not to assume. Always get the facts before deciding.

- Use positive thinking whenever possible.
  "Can't" never did anything!

- Take relaxation breaks. Try doing nothing for 30 minutes.

- Practice the "20 percent mess-up factor." Dare to screw up!

- Relax your standards. The world will not end if the grass doesn't get mowed this weekend, or if the sheets have to be changed on Sunday instead of Saturday.

- See the humor in life. As adults, we're often just winging it and playing at being grown-ups. We can be goofy – embrace it.

- Always set up contingency plans, "just in case."

- Turn off your phone and go for a long walk!

THE END - IS THIS TRIP REALLY OVER?

We are born and we die. We have little choice in either of those. However, the time between is filled to the brim with choices – and we live with the consequences of each choice we make. So be awake and choose wisely.

As I mentioned earlier, most individuals in their youth basically see themselves as immortal. As we get a bit older, we begin to realize the reality revealed in the old rhyme, "Tell me, tell me, will I die? Yes, you will, and so will I." Even though we all do know that someday we won't be around any longer, for many it's so far in the perceived future that we just can't wrap our heads around the idea. And as far as the time we have is concerned, nobody really knows. That's why it's so incredibly important that we embrace every day to the best of our ability, to enjoy that day, and not let anything or anyone interfere with the outcome, as long as we have the control to challenge that outcome.

In reality, what we fail to realize is that the only thing we do have control over in life is *quality*, not quantity. Yet maintaining the belief that life will continue to go on and on, individuals continually sabotage the quality of each day with the prospect that their "someday" life will be good and comfortable.

In "The Station," poet Robert Hastings wrote:

Tucked away in our subconscious is an idyllic vision.
We see ourselves on a long trip that spans the continent.
We are traveling by train...uppermost in our minds
is the final destination. On a certain day at a certain hour,
we will pull into the station. Bands will be playing and flags waving.

THE GOOD LIFE: A MATTER OF CHOICE

Once we get there, so many wonderful dreams will come true
and the pieces of our lives will fit together like a completed jigsaw puzzle.
How restlessly we pace the aisles, damning the minutes for loitering—
waiting, waiting, waiting for the station.
"When we reach the station that will be it!" we cry.
"When I'm 18."
"When I buy a new 450SL Mercedes Benz."
"When I put the last kid through college."
"When I have paid off the mortgage."
"When I get a promotion."
"When I reach the age of retirement, I shall live happily ever after!"
Sooner or later, we must realize there is no station,
no one place to arrive at once and for all.
The true joy of life is the trip. The station is only a dream.
It constantly outdistances us.
"Relish the moment" is a good motto.
It isn't the burdens of today that drive people mad.
It is the regrets over yesterday and the fear of tomorrow.
Regret and fear are twin thieves who rob us of today.
So, stop pacing the aisles and counting the miles.
Instead, climb more mountains, eat more ice cream,
go barefoot more often, swim more rivers, watch more sunsets,
laugh more, cry less.
Life must be lived as we go along.
The station will come soon enough.

It's important to identify the people that you have a strong emotional or spiritual connectedness with and ask yourself if you have expressed your feelings of appreciation for having those particular

The End – Is This Trip Really Over?

individuals in your life. Discuss those feelings with them and share your affection in ways that, if anything were to happen to any of those individuals, you would have a sense of closure and not feel, "I wish I would have."

From "If Tomorrow Never Comes," a poem published by Norma Cornett Marek in 1989:

> If I knew it would be the last time that I'd see you fall asleep, I would tuck you in more tightly, and pray the Lord your soul to keep.
>
> If I knew it would be the last time that I'd see you walk out the door, I would give you a hug and kiss, and call you back for just one more.
>
> If I knew it would be the last time I'd hear your voice lifted up in praise, I would tape each word and action, and play them back throughout my days.
>
> If I knew it would be the last time, I would spare an extra minute or two, to stop and say "I love you," instead of assuming you know I do.
>
> So just in case tomorrow never comes, and today is all I get, I'd like to say how much I love you, and I hope we never will forget. Tomorrow is not promised to anyone, young or old alike, and today may be the last chance you get to hold your loved one tight.
>
> So if you're waiting for tomorrow, why not do it today? For if tomorrow never comes, you'll surely regret the day that you didn't take that extra time for a smile, a hug, or a kiss,

and you were too busy to grant someone, what turned out to be their one last wish.

So hold your loved ones close today, and whisper in their ear, That you love them very much, and you'll always hold them dear. Take time to say "I'm sorry," "Please forgive me," "thank you" or "it's okay."

And if tomorrow never comes, you'll have no regrets about today.

We are responsible *100 percent of the time* for every thought, feeling, action and behavior. We may want to blame something or somebody else, but the reality is that we are the responsible party. Until we own this responsibility, we will find it very difficult to accept that we have the option to change whatever behavior, attitude, or emotion we may be experiencing. This is also why we may find ourselves continually giving our emotional credit card to a person or situation until, in most cases, we reach our emotional spending limit; and then, often figure out a way to increase it, even though the consequences may be emotional upsetness or physical ill health. Ask yourself...is what's upsetting to you now or what people feel about you now, going to make a difference in ten years? Or even next year?

Stop the scapegoating and blaming of others and avoid the assumptions that it's always someone else who has created the upsetness. If this were the last week, or the last year you'd be alive, would you do anything different? And, if so, what would you do? Now remember that

you don't actually have any concrete evidence that you will be here a year from now. Why not begin living your life as you would like to right now by making healthier and more positive choices, so that every day is a good trade?

Please understand. I don't mean to dwell on this, but are you going to die? Yes. Am I going to die? Sure. Get over it. This is not a question of if, or when – it's about the quality of how we live life today.

People fill calendars and shopping lists with to-do's, but rarely make the time to simply think. And be. They strive to build their 401k, buy a great car, increase the value of their house, become a hostage to all of the tech that's available, and spend so much time "doing" to create this or that, that they never take the time to enjoy what they already have.

In my travels, I have yet to see one weathered old gravestone identifying a person's net worth, the square footage of their house, the amount in their retirement account or a list of their possessions. In the end, we leave our name, the date of our birth and death, but little to identify how we lived. My family tells me that if they were to put an inscription on my grave marker besides my name, it would simply read, "He had a coupon." (They know me pretty well.)

Author James Barrie said, "God gave us memory so that we might have roses in December." How many of us near the end of this journey with our roses in December? Or as humorist Loretta LaRoche asked, "What will your tombstone say? 'Got it all done, dead anyway'?"

To enhance the quality of one's life and to empower one's self to get the most out of existence, living in the "here and now" is essential. Most people continue to bring things up from the past to defeat themselves in the present, and they anticipate the future in less than satisfying ways, which prevents them from dealing effectively with the here and now. Before one can blink, the here and now becomes part of the past and that can make for upsetness in not having done what one would have liked to accomplish.

THE GOOD LIFE: A MATTER OF CHOICE

As I've said to my clients many times, "It's not always easy to look in the mirror in the morning." To meet our own glance when we brush our teeth and to realize how responsible we really are for the kind of day it will be – for the trade we'll make of that day – can be very difficult. This serves to reinforce the importance of getting up each day and making that commitment to self, affirming that we really like the person we see and that we'll be the best we can be. The importance of not letting anything interfere with the quality of our day…and not willingly handing over our emotional credit card to anyone. Each day we should also vow to do whatever we can to enhance the life quality of those who are close to us. This helps make the here and now a more special experience, instead of time lost. It was Alfred Souza, writer and philosopher, who said, "For a long time it seemed to me that life was about to begin – real life. But there was always some obstacle in the way, something to be gotten through first, some unfinished business, time to still be served, a debt to be paid. Then life would begin. At last it dawned on me that these obstacles were my life."

When people churn up the past, they defeat themselves in the present. They're creating worry, emotional upset, physiological stress, and most importantly, the inability to deal effectively and positively with what's in front of them. Sure, if one makes plans for the future, that can be wonderful, but to worry or obsess in negativistic terms about the future is one more way we have of dealing a blow to the quality of our life in our today.

It's not how long we live, but how we live. It's important to take the time to reflect in terms of what quality, or lack thereof, one has in life. Many people have discovered this and tried to pass it on, but so many times the message often falls on deaf ears. As Abraham Lincoln is aphoristically credited as saying, "In the end, it's not the years in your life that count. It's the life in your years."

So will you look back and say you wish you had the last ten, twenty or thirty years to live over again because they were wonderful? Or, like most people, will you say you wish you had the last ten, twenty or thirty years to live over again because you would certainly live them differently? It's a sad thing to hear someone say the latter, when, in reality, most of us possess the power and control to have the former be our truth. And here's a way to respond to excuses like "I'm too old to change," or "that's just the way I am," or "that's the way our family has always been." Tell the person to raise their arm. When they do, ask if they could have done that five minutes ago, or five minutes from now. When they answer yes, remind them that they can't prove what they might have done in the past, and that they can't show what they will do in the future. The only reality we truly have is *now*. If we can raise an arm in the now, we can also choose to create change in the now, for a better life and a better experience.

Many of us keep our heads in the proverbial sands of "I'm going to continue living as-is" instead of gaining insight and a healthy awareness from all those who have come before us. Through the wisdom of philosophers, writers, clinicians and even our own friends and relatives, we are presented with choices about healthier ways to think and behave that can only enhance the quality of our lives, fulfilling each day in an eventful and gratifying manner. The reality is that we are only – and always – one second away from the ability to make a new choice.

As we've discussed, most people delude themselves into believing that they will have time to do things differently or make whatever changes are necessary to enhance their lives in a positive outcome. Unfortunately, none of us have any inside knowledge that supports the comfort of thinking that there will always be another year to do things differently. That is why the good life is a matter of choice and those choices need to be made now, not postponed to a later date that may never materialize. Many of us go through life avoiding risk and being fearful of making mistakes. We journey through our lives carrying with us the proverbial hot water bottle and parachute to always be safe. Writer James Joyce said, "Mistakes are the portals of discovery." The more we are willing to test our adequacy and do battle with our fears, and take whatever risks are necessary to gratify our needs, the more fulfilling and satisfying our lives as we know them will be – no matter what the length or what adversities confront us. Choices are available to us throughout our lives. When we challenge our negative scripting, replace self-defeating statements from our private critics and combat our fears by dealing with the outcomes and not the "might-be's," we find we have chosen a life worthy of happy, satisfying reflections instead of shouldas, couldas and wish-I-wouldas.

In "The Prophet," Khalil Gibran wrote:

And the treasure of your infinite depths would be revealed to your eyes.
But let there be no scales to weigh your unknown treasure;
And seek not the depths of your knowledge with staff or sounding line.
For self is a sea boundless and measureless.

If only we would listen more carefully to the words of the great minds throughout history, and implement what they have encouraged us to understand and do differently, how much more joyful and fulfilling our lives – and the lives of those around us – could be.

Although there are sometimes circumstances that make change difficult, "difficult" is not "impossible." Difficulties only make things take a little longer. Once we make the choice and allow determination to prevail within our physical limits, anything is possible.

Time is precious. We know this – but we continue to rush the time or negotiate with ourselves in ways that are so counterintuitive.

When we're young, we hate to wait for anticipated events, like school vacations, and when they finally arrive they are over so quickly. When we get older, many of us continue to live in this same way – enduring a less than satisfactory quality of life because we are only waiting for the weekend or that two-week vacation. Instead we could (and should!) be realizing that each day we awake, there are a myriad of quality experiences just waiting for us, emotionally healthy choices to sample throughout the day we've been given. For those of us who are at the age when the body sometimes feels as if it were assembled like an Erector set, or our wrinkles make us look like it's time for Halloween (no costume required), or the rest of our parts need a good deal of assistance just to be able to hear or see or walk, we can still choose real quality, despite all of those inconveniences. We can still enjoy each day to the fullest, living as a testimony for the others in our lives and encouraging them to begin choosing quality at whatever age they are – living the good life by example.

The title of this book, *The Good Life: A Matter of Choice*, presents exactly what it indicates. That no matter our age or situation, we always have choices available. My great hope is that each of us will choose to be introspective and committed to making healthy choices for optimum quality in our lives.

Remember, there is no age restriction for enhancing one's quality of life. Just because a person is older and may not be involved in the same activities that they used to enjoy, does not mean that there are no other options available. Unfortunately, many older individuals also perceive themselves as limited or even irrelevant, viewing life through that same filter that society has insinuated upon them – not willing to challenge that scripting.

A previous quote by Satchel Paige asked, "How old would you be if you didn't know how old you are?" I think that speaks volumes about how many of us really are capable of doing a great deal to enhance the quality of our lives, yet we end up doing no more than what Zane Grey described as the cowboy riding fence. Back in the days of the Old West, when a cowboy was seen as no longer able to perform more rigorous tasks, he would be sent out to mend fences along the vast perimeter of a ranch. And ultimately, he would be found slumped over the saddle, reinforcing the old expression, "He died with his boots on."

At the end of our physical journey comes death, and whatever that means to each of us. It's a word most people don't wish to discuss for many reasons. There is fear of the unknown, the tremendous sadness of leaving those individuals we are emotionally and spiritually connected with, the reluctance of terminating a life that may not have been fully lived, or whatever else a person feels who may be reluctantly awaiting their disconnection from this world.

As Ashleigh Brilliant in the cartoon *Pot-Shots* jokingly stated, "No use getting too involved in life, I'm only here for a limited time."

I'll say it again. Death is the one certainty we have. This is why it's so incredibly important to value each day and maintain the quality of our life without focusing on the quantity. What we have is control over the *quality* of our life, and not the *quantity*. Don't be a person who continually sabotages the quality of each day without realizing that they always possess the control to change those aspects of life which are uncomfortable or not working.

Your someday life is available to you now.

When working with older or ill patients, one thing I hear to be a major concern is not being available for various individuals and important events after we've gone, such as a graduation, a wedding or birth. Something you can do to feel more empowered in this respect is to sit down and write out a brief note to each individual – so you can still be "present" at those particular times even if you're no longer available to express your thoughts in person.

It's also quite gratifying to make contact with people you have not talked to in a while, just to express the importance or the quality they brought to your life. Tell them how much you enjoyed your relationship with them. Whatever comes about as a result of this contact, at least you've shared your truth.

If at all possible, we must try to do those things we tell ourselves we would like to do but don't make the time to do. We should use those things we set aside for special occasions – the sterling flatware, crystal or the good china. Use it every day. This moment in your life is the most special occasion you will encounter. And the next moment will be the most special occasion. And as other events occur, those will be the most special occasions, too. Dust less; read more. Listen to music. Sit on the deck or elsewhere and just be. Go for a walk and enjoy the world around you. Appreciate what you experience and everything that touches your life.

We feel, especially if we are fortunate enough to have good health, that we have plenty of time to do good things, but situations can occur that we don't anticipate. That's why it's important to both embrace the moment and be prepared. It's no different than having company over for dinner and being prepared for what guests may want to drink or eat. We go to the grocery store with a list of items needed for meals in the following week; we lay out clothes the night before in preparation for the next day; we do lots of things every day to prepare ourselves for our routines or special events. Yet end-of-life – a complete certainty – is something so many of us are ill-prepared for, as evidenced by how many of us postpone writing up living wills, powers of attorney, and other end-of-life requests. So just get yourself as prepared as you can be, and then get on with living.

A memorable cartoon by Jules Feiffer shows two individuals sitting across from one another. One is reading the paper and one is holding a drink and after several scenes of this, the husband asks his

THE GOOD LIFE: A MATTER OF CHOICE

spouse, "Do you believe in life after death?" Two more scenes go by and the wife answers, "What do you call this?" Although it's a cartoon and meant to be humorous, so many times this is the reality of our lives – living in such a disconnected routine and a lifestyle lacking in quality, playfulness or gratification, that when the idea of life after death comes up, this is the feeling we're left with.

Like Ashleigh Brilliant in another of his *Pot-Shots* cartoons said, "Communication with the dead is only a little more difficult than communication with some of the living." Susan Ertz, an American author in the early 1900's, also stated, "Millions long for immortality who do not know what to do with themselves on a rainy Sunday afternoon."

Whatever one decides to do in preparation for end-of-life, the most important thing is making good choices and good trades on a daily basis, and making positive connections and interactions with those who are important and significant in our lives while we're here now.

People spend time and money sending flowers to a funeral home, planning a memorial service, and writing an obituary in celebration of a life. Instead, who not consider doing all this while your loved ones are still alive and can appreciate these kind gestures, your affection and the words that honor the value they have brought forth in your life? Think about how well we actually communicate to the most important people in our lives. Let's do a better job of delivering those messages of appreciation for their existence – don't put it off.

Remember that as you go through life, you should feel empowered to take more risks, challenge more fears, and see it all as an adventure. An adventure that we need to invest our total being in so that when the time finally does come to an end, we will have worn out this body, and our time, in a productive and wholly satisfying manner.

Someone once said that death is just nature's way of telling you, "Hey, you're not alive anymore," and, artist, inventor, and philosopher Leonardo daVinci said, "A well spent day brings happy sleep, so life well used brings happy death." Although he doesn't say it in so many words, he certainly underscores the importance of making healthy decisions and good trades every day, so that the good life – at whatever stage you find yourself – is yours for the choosing.

WHAT ARE YOU WAITING FOR?

This is difficult work for most of us. We would like to experience a great deal more in life, but we expend so much time and energy going through it with that hot water bottle and parachute to protect us from our own self-talk. We respond to perceived fears without validation, which creates all the roadblocks.

If we would get up each day and challenge ourselves to be the best we can be, whatever that may mean, and really like the person we are, making the changes when necessary in order to improve the quality of our lives, it would certainly provide the motivation and positive energy to embark on whatever journey might be out there for us. We cannot allow the perceptions or behaviors of others to interfere in our pursuit of a quality life.

We have a tendency to put things off when we're in good health because we believe in that sense of immortality. However, the only reality we ever have is the here and now. Like the stone once tossed that can never be retrieved, and the word once said that can never be taken back, time that is lost can never be recovered.

Imagine life as a pie. Ask yourself which piece you are really enjoying now, which piece you might dig into soon, and which pieces are being wrapped up for another day, a better time or a different opportunity?

Your only opportunity for change is making that choice today. The Good Life you're looking for is the choice that's available to you right now.

What are you waiting for?

THE GOOD LIFE: A MATTER OF CHOICE

AFTERWORD

I was born and raised in Grand Rapids, Michigan. My mother had four sons – each five years apart. I was the youngest. Our home was blue collar. My Dad worked at a service station and my Mom played piano in a bar at night. Working hard was in the family DNA and even as a little kid, I always found a way to work (read: hustle some money).

My parents signed for me to go into the Air Force when I was seventeen years old. I passed up flight school and chose training as a laboratory technician/medic. After returning from Korea and discharge from the Air Force, I took a job at Blodgett Memorial Hospital and eventually I ran an independent medical lab for a group of internists.

When I was working, I was also a full-time student and finished a B.A. in psychology from Aquinas College in 1967. This allowed me to become employed as a psychologist by the State of Michigan in an aftercare program brought about by the closing of the big state psychiatric hospitals (Public Act 54). While I was involved in that job, I finished my master's degree in psychology and completed a specialist's degree at Western Michigan University.

In 1969, I was a member of the Wyoming, Michigan, Junior Chamber of Commerce – the JCs. There was a community desire to provide support to teens during that tumultuous time.

ACT (The Advisory Center for Teens) was born, and I became the executive director. I got a PhD in psychology from Western Colorado University in 1973. They allowed me to use the PhD staff at Western Michigan so I could complete and defend my thesis locally. ACT erected and dedicated a new-from-the-ground-up facility in 1975. I went into private practice that year.

In my practice, I specialize in treatment of individuals and do a great deal of relationship and family therapy as a licensed Marriage and Family Therapist. I also taught a course at Aquinas College which I developed, called, "Taking Charge of Your Life."

Various individuals asked if I had written a book and told me I should write one.

A degree wasn't the only thing I got from my psychology major at Aquinas. I also found my wife, Barb, a fellow psych major. We married early, had two daughters early, and have lived many of the same the trials, tribulations and missteps of most folks. Now, more than 50 years and four grandchildren later, we have hindsight, experience, adventures and love. And a book.

We're not done yet.

THE GOOD LIFE